EXTINCTION

Other Books by the Author:

A life Well Lived
Words Matter

EXTINCTION

ROBERT BYRUM

Extinction
Copyright © 2023 by Robert Byrum. All rights reserved.

No part of this publication may be reproduced, stored in a retrieval system or transmitted in any way by any means, electronic, mechanical, photocopy, recording or otherwise without the prior permission of the author except as provided by USA copyright law.

The opinions expressed by the author are not necessarily those of URLink Print and Media.

1603 Capitol Ave., Suite 310 Cheyenne, Wyoming USA 82001
1-888-980-6523 | admin@urlinkpublishing.com

URLink Print and Media is committed to excellence in the publishing industry.

Book design copyright © 2023 by URLink Print and Media. All rights reserved.

Published in the United States of America

Library of Congress Control Number: 2023916053
ISBN 978-1-68486-503-1 (Paperback)
ISBN 978-1-68486-510-9 (Digital)

23.07.23

Dedicated: To the children of the world who will have to suffer for our mistakes

"We are the product of 4.5 billion years of fortuitous, slow biological evolution. There is no reason to think that the evolutionary process has stopped. Man is a transitional animal. He is not the climax of creation."
— Carl Sagan 1934–1996

"Men will come and go, leaving behind only tiny scars to mark their passing. This as it has always been and always will be. They will one day disappear as the mountains have been eroded, the glaciers melted, and the planets rearranged. We are only a speck in time, only an instant in the constant evolution of change."
— Author Unknown

CONTENTS

Extinction 11
The Present... 19
Climate Change and Weather 25
Species.. 45
Financial... 49
Energy 53
Migration 57
Health 59
Plastics and Pollution 61
Infrastructure 65
Arctic Permafrost and Methane Gas.......................... 73
The Oceans 79
Politics and Reality.. 93
Climate Summit Meeting 115
Reflections 123

EXTINCTION

Can we save the planet and ourselves? The environmental devastation that the world is experiencing today, including record-breaking temperatures, wildfires in the American West, Turkey, Greece; historic flooding in Western Europe, the East Coast of the United States, the Pacific Northwest, and central China; and the drought-driven famines exceed anything we could have imagined even a year ago. Just breathing the air and drinking the water is a health hazard for millions of people around the globe. Our oceans have changed and become polluted and warmer endangering people's livelihoods.

How will future generations view our actions if we fail to act now, as we have not done in the past? What will they say about us, knowing we spent billions of dollars exploring space and left the earth behind? We are warming on a grand scale, the result of our use of fossil fuels is a blanket tucked around the entire earth keeping us warm or turning us slowly to roast. Today we are roasting on a giant spit; how well done we will get is up to us.

There are two elements that are the major cause of our current toasting: carbon dioxide and methane. For over 300,000 years, carbon dioxide in the atmosphere had been stable averaging between 230 parts per million (ppm) and 250 ppm as determined from fossil records and ice cores taken from the Antarctic glaciers. Today that level is 415 ppm and climbing. In the past 800,000 years, the level of CO_2 has never been as high as what we are experiencing today.

Only when man arrived on the scene and started the development of today's industrial society, two hundred years ago, did the level of CO_2 in the atmosphere begin to rise, starting the warming process that continues today. Just two hundred years! In hardly a wink in time we have changed the world. The current level of CO_2 in the atmosphere will continue to increase every year as we continue to ignore the hazards and continue burning fossil fuels.

Over the planet's history there have been many extinctions occurring eons of time before man came on the scene. Is that changing, is the process of extinction done, or are we on the edge of a cliff dangling one foot into space and not realizing how close we are of slipping into eternity? Man has never suffered a major extinction. He did not contribute until now; he did not exist.

Humanity is clearly capable of causing its own extinction by nuclear war and climate change caused by our own activities and our ability to destroy or collapse ecosystems. The insidious thing about extinction is that it tends to be gradual over long time periods, often leading a domino effect in which one event stresses one or more species, leading to other events that destroy many more. Such multiple events eventually lead to the final verdict.

Our modern human existence and history on this big rock has been very short in geological time. Several million years ago, early man started his long voyage to the present. It has just been over the last 10,000 years that we have evolved rapidly in the evolution process to arrive at where we are today. A mere tiny grain of sand in time compared to the 4.5 billion years since the planet's birth. To get an idea of the significance of our existence, extend your arm out from your shoulder to the tips of your fingernails, have someone take an emery board and lightly brush your fingernail. The tiny amount removed represents human history, the rest of your arm represents the planet's long existence. We are but bit players occupying a very small chapter in the history of evolution. How many pages will our episode contain? For another vivid example of just how short our time has been on the planet, view the Washington Monument in Washington, DC, place a thin piece of paper on its pointed top; its thickness is us.

Over geological times, there have been five major catastrophic extinctions that are defined as the loss of fifty percent (50%) or more of all life on the planet. These extinctions normally occurred gradually; it was a slow process occurring over millions of years that allowed some plants and other living organisms to adapt to the changing conditions

Extinction

and survive. The exception was the last event that occurred 65 million years ago caused by a climatic impact of a meteorite that exterminated the dinosaurs and many other life forms.

Extinction has always been the rule, not the exception. More than 99% of the four billion species that have evolved on earth over its long history are now gone. During the last five centuries, 900 species have been lost. There are several causes that can contribute to a species going extinct, including habitat destruction, climate change, and disease. Epidemics have been the cause of extinction of large populations of humans and animals on earth in the past. Before the arrival of Europeans on our continent, it is estimated that there were 100 million Native Americans. In just one hundred years they were reduced to a population of approximately five million caused primarily by diseases such as cholera for which they had no natural immunity. Lack of genetic diversity is another—when a species starts decreasing, the gene pool of the species grows smaller and eventually there is a loss of genetic diversity.

Scientist agree that species go extinct primarily as a result of changes in their environment and we are one of those species. Severe changes in the environment result in a slow loss or change in the habitat necessary for species survival and eventually the damage is irreversible. Global extinction is the elimination of a particular species or many species everywhere in the world, but it need not be one hundred percent.

The five major global extinction periods as defined by the scientific study of fossil history:
- Ordovician - 440 million years ago (mya)
- Late Devonian - 364mya
- Permian - Triassic - 250mya
- Triassic - Jurassic - 200mya
- Cretaceous - 65mya

Ordovician Mass Extinction:

Period - 440mya

Loss - 85% of all living species eliminated.

Suspected cause - Continental Drift - Life was in its very early stages of development. The first known small basic life forms had started to developed approximately 3.6 billion years ago. By the late Ordovician period early larger aquatic life had existed along with some land species.

The cause of the extinction is thought to have been the shifting around the globe of the moving continents, causing drastic climate change along with violent volcanic activity, an ice age that nearly covered the entire earth and then rapid warming created conditions species could not adapt rapidly enough to survive. There were very few surviving aquatic life forms left to increase the necessary oxygen levels so new species could evolve. The oceans developed and contained the large majority of the remaining life and from them oxygen was created forming the foundation of future life. The land contained very little life; it was barren.

Devonian Mass Extinction:

Period - 375mya

Loss - 80% of all living species

Suspected cause - Lack of oxygen in the oceans created massive deaths; there was considerably less oxygen available than today. The quick cooling of Earth's surface; massive volcanic eruptions and meteor strikes. The earth was a very violent place. The amount of greenhouse gas in the atmosphere was depleted rapidly by the increasing land plants that absorbed it allowing temperatures to drop rapidly. The earth's heat-retaining blanket was removed, allowing heat to escape into the atmosphere. Land species were wiped out; aquatic life fared somewhat better.

Permian Mass Extinction:
Period - 250mya
Loss - 96%
Cause - Unknown, possibly asteroid strikes, volcanic activity climate change and microbes.

This was the largest of all known extinctions. The earth came very close to becoming a dead planet again. Its cause is not known. Some believe it may have been caused by a number of events, including massive volcanic activity along with asteroids that sent deadly methane gas into the atmosphere around the earth resulting in a decrease in oxygen, changing the climate that suffocated life forms. It would be a long time, as much as 80 million years before those species that were left recovered.

Triassic - Jurassic Mass Extinction:
Period - 200mya
Loss - more than 50% of all life
Cause - Massive volcanic activity with basalt gas flooding the atmosphere causing global climate change. Changing sea levels and chemicals levels in the ocean.

This fourth major event occurred over a long time period of 18 million years with small events accelerating the loss. It was caused primarily by volcanic activity that sent gases into the atmosphere creating climate change.

Cretaceous K-T Mass Extinction:
Period - 65mya
Loss - Nearly 75% of all living species
Cause - Extreme asteroid or meteor impact

This latest large event wiped out the dinosaurs, although they were not the only species to go extinct. The well-documented cause of this event was a major asteroid impact that sent millions of tons of debris into the air and around the earth effectually blocking out the sun and producing an ongoing winter, drastically changing the climate of the entire planet and killing the plant life the animals depended on.

From a study published in the Proceedings of the National Academy of Science:

During the Late Triassic Pluvial Episode (CPE), 232–234 million years ago, volcanoes drove the increase in global temperatures and humidity that created conditions that caused intense rainfall known as "mega monsoons," which had a considerable impact in promoting the development of animal and plant life. Major climate changes caused a large disturbance of the carbon cycle to more humid conditions. Volcanic eruptions can greatly alter the global carbon cycle and drive the evolutionary process. It takes a relative long period of high volcanic activity. During this time, the dinosaurs began to evolve into ecological dominance that lasted for 150 million years. This period in Earth's history had a major impact on the evolution of land ecosystems and animal and plant life including ours.

AOL News, The Web. 9/29/2021 Bird Species Declared Extinct: The government has exhausted efforts to find the 23 species they have listed and warn that climate change, on the top of other pressures, could make such disappearances more common as the warming planet adds to the hazards facing imperiled plants and wildlife. The factors behind the disappearances vary from too much development, water pollution, logging, and competition from invasive species. In each case, humans were the ultimate cause. It was said that the toll of extinction would have been much higher without the Endangered Species Act.

Microsoft News, The Web, 7/28/2021: The Columbia River is currently 71 degrees. That's 3 degrees above levels that are safe for salmon. Also, on Sacramento River in California, officials expect nearly all the juvenile salmon could die this summer due to extreme heat and low water flows. Unless there is more free flowing cold water available, they may go extinct. They cannot handle the impact of the dams and warming water caused climate change.

Extinction

Dead Forest, I.R. 12/13/2021: A combination of drought and heat waves that led to the massive wildfires that ravaged southeastern Australia in 2019 and 2020 have left up to 60% of the trees that escaped the fires dead. Western Sydney University researchers found that even species that are "superbly adapted" to Australia's harsh conditions had died. The record heat and drought were just too much for many common varieties. If the trees don't grow back, their absence threatens the ability of food and other resources for insects, birds, and other species.

Covid-19 is the extinction of reality for many people in this country today. They are dying needlessly because they refuse to accept proven behaviors that would have saved their lives. These are the same people who proclaim the virus is a hoax and declare that climate change does not exist. With climate change increasing nobody, including us, is left off the endangered species list.

> "When the last individual of a race of living things breathes no more, another heaven and Mother Earth must pass before such a one can be again."
> – William Beebe

THE PRESENT

Mother Nature is the greatest terrorist of them all. Piss her off with global warming, overpopulation, pollution etc., and she will bite us back as severely as the greatest weapons of mass destruction. It is already happening and she is getting mad.

Are we living today in the midst of the sixth extinction? Will humans survive and for how long? That has yet to be determined, but we must remember that humans played no part in contributing to any previous mass extinctions. We were not there. How much are we contributing to a future one?

There are many types of extinctions. We normally think of them as catastrophic worldly events, but they can occur as a more personal tragedy. If you die, you are extinct, all of your individuality is destroyed, your quirks your personality, there is no one else like you, you are gone forever. Natural tragedies are extinctions of a way of life for millions of people today. When your life changes, when there is no hope in the future to return to your previous way of life, your past has become extinct. There also can be temporary extinctions. When your house is destroyed by wildfires, hurricanes, or other national disasters, now caused more frequently by climate change, that can be temporary, but you are still the victim of that loss that may continue for some time. When your home is lost along with all your items of memory, they no longer exist; they have gone extinct.

Extinction can also mean: Of New Ideas, Reason, Honesty, Common Sense, The Rule of Law, Of Love with Hate, Knowledge by Ignorance, Wisdom by Stupidity, Freedom by Anarchy. Unfortunately, there can be no extinction of stupidly; it is too well established.

Today we have glorified the stupidity of our leaders that will never produce collective wisdom. This is a step towards the decline of our society into the throes of national upheaval.

Plato in 380 BC, described that kind of individual that we see in politics all too frequently today.

"Bringing home Insolence, Anarchy, Waste, and Impudence, those resplendent divinities crowned with garlands, whose praise they sing under flattering names: Insolence they call good breeding, Anarchy freedom, Waste magnificence and Impudence a manly spirit. Every now and then they leap to their feet to say or do whatever comes into their head."

The thread of life on which we all depend is very thin. In the oceans, most of the entire food chain depends on just two of our smallest life forms—Phytoplankton and Zooplankton on which small fish such as anchovies, herring, and sardines feed and which the larger species depend on for their existence. Their loss or reduction would cripple that ocean's ecosystem. As photosynthesis is essential to plant life on earth and to all living things that use the oxygen, these two small living ocean organisms must survive. Are they being harmed by the increased warming of the oceans by climate change, pollution, increased acidification of our oceans' waters, and the additions of microplastics?

Photosynthesis is the process that all plants use to take energy from the sun and carbon dioxide (CO_2) from the atmosphere to generate oxygen. At sea level, our current atmosphere contains approximately 21% of oxygen, the largest component is hydrogen with other small trace amounts of other gases and water vapor. As we have all experienced as we go higher, the amount of oxygen decreases. One of the major causes of past extinctions has been the loss in the ability of plants to produce oxygen.

We as humans exhibit the same process as plants only in reverse. We take in oxygen that the plants provide as we breath and exhale carbon dioxide. Imagine the amount of carbon dioxide seven billion people on earth exhale into the atmosphere every day.

The volcanism that occurred during the past mass extinctions was a source of high CO_2 concentrations that is known from carbon-dated fossils; that rate of increase of CO_2 input that was determined at those times was similar to the rate of increase we are seeing today. During a mega-volcano eruption or a large meteor striking the earth, millions of tons of dust, ash, toxic gasses, including huge amounts of carbon dioxide, and other elements were sent into the high atmosphere and circulated around the world blocking out the sun from the plants, creating a continuing winter and disrupting their ability to produce this vital life sustaining element. This condition can exist for thousands of years.

Carbon dioxide in the atmosphere then surges for the lack of a way for it to be removed, killing all living things. It takes a very large event, like what occurred in Yellowstone National Park's massive volcanic eruption or the event that destroyed the dinosaurs to achieve this, but they have happened in the past and will happen again in the future. Hopefully, not during man's existence. Smaller volcanic eruptions that happen around the world almost daily, emit large amounts of gasses, including CO_2 and methane that are dispersed and held in the atmosphere.

The earth is not static; it is constantly changing; it always has and always will. It is still making mountains and destroying them by the erosion effects of the sun, wind, and water. The Himalayas will one day be the size of the low rolling Appalachian Mountains that exist today along the East Coast of North America as those mountains were once the size of the Himalayas. Over hundreds of millions of years, these mountains have eroded to their present state. The continents are still moving about on Earth's surface and some oceans are getting smaller and some larger. Fortunately, most of the time these changes are small and very slow, occurring over millions of years, but they can also happen very fast and be catastrophic.

On Earth today, changes are occurring more rapidly caused by human activity, than at any time in the recent geological past. Think of what we have done to our environment in just the last two hundred years since the start of the industrial revolution. We have degraded our water, our air, and our soil at a rate that has never happened before. This must give us serious cause for alarm.

The recent report of the Intergovernmental Panel on Climate Change (IPOC) was described as "code red" for the future of humanity. "The earth is dangerously close to running out of time to stop a climate change catastrophe," the UK government's climate chief Alok Sharnia has said. "We cannot afford to wait two years, five years, ten years; this is the moment." Warming signs are occurring on every continent and region with scorching temperatures, biodiversity loss, polluted air, water, and natural space. The oceans will continue to warm and become more acidic. Mountain and polar glaciers will continue melting for the coming decades and centuries."

Unfortunately, he did not condemn governments for allowing more fossil fuel projects. All of the CO_2 now in the atmosphere will remain there for hundreds of years and cannot be easily reduced. Any amount currently being added will only make the conditions more severe. Levels of molecular hydrogen (H_2), a very powerful greenhouse gas, have also surged in modern times. Air samples trapped in drilled ice cores of Antarctic ice indicate H_2 has increased 70% over the course of the twentieth century. H_2 can impact the distribution of methane and ozone in the atmosphere.

10/12/2021, Newsweek, The Web: The Middle East now produces almost as much greenhouse gas as the European Union, according to the Associated Press. George Zittis, a scientist at the Cyprus Institutes of Climate and Atmosphere Research Center said: "We need to completely decarbonize, even go negative in greenhouse gas emissions." Zittis also said that governments in the Middle East have to make the switch to renewable energy within the next two decades to avert potentially "irreversible effects" such as desertification. He also warned of possible mass migrations from countries in the Middle East as water gets scarce and temperatures rise.

Heat Islands: Heat stored in buildings and other man-made objects like roads is causing nearly one quarter of the world's population that live in cities to suffer increased health hazards and economic hardships caused by global heating. Researchers write in the Proceedings of the National Academy of Science that, as metropolitan areas grow larger, they will become even greater heat traps. During the past forty years, hundreds of million people have moved from rural areas to cities in search a better life. The increasing heat worsens pre-existing health conditions and the ability to work, the report says. About forty major cities in the US have seen exposure to extreme heat grow rapidly, mainly in the Gulf Coast states from Florida to Texas.

The US has had 265 weather disasters that caused at least 1 billion dollars in damage, or more since 1992, including 18 so far this year in 2021. Those disasters have caused 11,990 deaths and cost $1.8 trillion dollars. From 1980 to 1992, the US averaged 3 of those billion-dollar weather disasters year. Since 1993 the country has averaged nine a year. During the four hottest months of the year the added heat from climate change is responsible for 0.58% of the global deaths. That amounts to 100,000 heat deaths a year for twenty-nine years. It is estimated that figure will raise to 250,000 a year by 2030.

From 1993 to 2019, the world put more than 885 billion tons of CO_2 into the atmosphere that will remain there for hundreds of years. This meeting in Scotland may well be the last shot we have in preserving the earth, not as we know it now, but at least give it a chance for a future. We can talk and talk and throw money at it, but in no way will that ever make a difference in the conditions we have already created that are leading to the continued warming. We cannot buy Mother Nature off. We are on a super highway speeding past the 2 degrees Celsius that we dare not exceed. The longer we delay action the more doors slam shut as we run out of options; more devastation, and then it becomes too late for some places on Earth and many ecosystems and species to recover, of which we are one.

Dedicated to the youth of today and the significance of the changes in your world; why should you worry or care?
1. The oceans are not rising fast.

2. The severe storms are not affecting me.
3. Oh, so in 2100 the world will change due to climate change. So, what, that's a long way off.
4. You are 20; soon, faster than you think, you will be 70. What will your world be like then? Will you really try to understand what's happening now or will you live one party after another until the party is over and the reality of what has been occurring hits you in the face. You live today in a wonderland of material toys: TV, iPads, Twitter, and on and on. For how long? Realize they are just toys; new ones will come and today's trinkets will fade. Your world is warming today at a rate not experienced in the last 10,000 years. At least realize what is happening and possibly dedicate yourself to do something about it.

CLIMATE CHANGE AND WEATHER

"Wisdom cries aloud in the streets; in the market she raises her voice: How long O simple ones, will you love being simple? How long will scoffers delight in their scoffing and fools hate knowledge?"
– Proverbs 1.20

Pope Francis on Saturday called on lawmakers worldwide to overcome "the narrow confines" of partisan politics to quickly reach consensus on fighting climate change.

Are we humans the "frog in the pan?" Do we lack the capacity to feel the water boiling (climate change) and take action and jump or are we destined to boil slowly away in our own caldron? Are we croaking "economic growth, economic growth" until we boil? As we rightly increase wind and solar power, do we decrease their overall benefits by promoting growth for growth's sake? When will we attack all emissions? Until we do, it's a zero-sum game and the earth will lose.

"The long-term trend is very clear. And it's because of us. And it's not going away until we stop increasing the amount of carbon dioxide in the atmosphere," Gavin Schmidt, a NASA climate scientist said after data showed that 2021 was the fifth hottest year on record. Death Valley, in California reached 130 degrees, the planet's hottest temperature on record.

This work is not intended to be a detailed discussion on climate change, rather it is intended to focus on where we are possibly headed in the future and to inform the reader about the specific events that are now already occurring on the planet. Climate change obviously is a major player, but unless we understand the many changes that it is producing, and the many varied and damaging ways it is altering the world today, repeating climate change, climate change is an empty shell.

The term "Climate Change" has become a generic phrase, referring generally to what is occurring to the weather around the globe. But what are the actual effects of this change? We see and hear the phrase discussed by the media, the politicians, and by the general public. It is used to explain a current and future crisis in a way that doesn't explain much. What does it really mean? It vaguely refers to something that is happening or will happen, but it is not just happening; it's being caused by us. Until we define and study some of the actual and numerous and tragic events today that we humans are responsible for, its meaning cannot be fully appreciated.

If we have learned anything from the COVID-19 virus, let alone the present and coming climate crisis, it's that the systems that support modern civilizations are brittle. It is obvious that the potential of a large meteor event is much less a hazard to Earth than the virus and global warming. It's a matter of time, and time is certainly on our side for such a climatic occurrence. But time is not on our side for an equally disastrous result due to inaction and ignorance to what's occurring today.

Simplistic climate change corrections are attractive to the public—like planting trees—but will they work in time and are they effective? Trees take decades or longer to fully realize their capacity to remove carbon. That's why the destruction of large areas of trees in the Amazon Jungle is so tragic. It would require an absurd amount of land to plant enough trees to make a large impact on the climate. And we must remember that when trees die, burn, or are harvested, they release their stored carbon back into the atmosphere.

All the forest fires burning in the Western United States and around the world are releasing carbon into an ever-increasing warmer world. Fires in the Mediterranean basin, North America, and Siberia this year have resulted in the highest level of carbon emissions into the atmosphere from wildfires ever recorded during summer in the

Northern Hemisphere. According to a report by Europe's Earth Observation Agency, Copernicus, 1.3 billion tons of CO_2 were released in July and 1.4 billion tons in August. Almost a third came from fires in Russia. In Russia's Sakha Republic, satellites registered a new record on August 3, 2021 when emissions for the day were more than double those of June, July, and August of last year combined. With the continued burning, forest fires are causing threats to watersheds as they destroy trees and cover that control water flow, increasing floods and mudslides that contaminate streams, rivers, and lakes.

Business Insider, The Web 11/10/2021. Wildfires in California and Siberia are sending soot into the atmosphere that is landing in the Arctic and adding to the melt of the polar ice. The soot, called black carbon, settles on the ice and darkens it, absorbing heat and preventing solar heat from reflecting back into the atmosphere.

Solar and wind energy and producing facilities certainly are the answer and they can be constructed rapidly. But the problem is the infostructure those facilities need to hold and transfer the energy they produce to the locations where it is used. It can take up to ten years to build and install these facilities. The building of nuclear energy facilities that can produce clean energy can take much longer to overcome political, economic, and social restrictions. Do we have the time? But even nuclear power is not clean, its used residue will last thousands of years as a toxic hazard.

Climate change is not the entire issue, the extinction of life on our planet and its ecosystems and how and where that may be occurring should be our major interest now and in the future. It is the multiple events that will happen over a long time frame and how they might be controlled is what should govern our actions. Certainly, controlling future heat-producing emissions is absolutely essential, but it is not enough. Today's heat will continue to effect changes to the environment for hundreds of years. We must lengthen our thinking and consider the consequences of not acting long term. Setting arbitrary dates like 2050 as a point for the final solution will not work.

Global warming and climate change might be better defined as the many insidious actions of a thousand damaging activities they cause by slowly destroying the planet as they effectively erode its life-sustaining substance towards eventual extinction.

It is the warming of the seas; the destruction of our forests by fire, drought, and man's activities; the worldwide melting of the glaciers; the loss of the Arctic sea ice; melting of the Greenland ice cap; early snowmelt and runoff; wildlife habitat destruction; extensive destructive forest fires; global conflicts; disruption of agriculture; fisheries destruction; stronger and more numerous hurricanes, storms, and tornados; increased intense rainfall and flooding; droughts; ocean acidification; loss of ocean oxygen; coral damage and destruction; increased insect populations, disease and health impacts; immigration; and melting of the Arctic permafrost. The planet is in trouble; what have we wrought?

In ecology there is no such thing as an action of one thing that does not effect changes in others. It is all linked; all parts of ecosystems are connected. It may well be that each of those episodes listed above will trigger other changes that today we are not aware of.

There are included below a number of different recorded events that I hope will help clarify and explain the extent and variety of some of the significant changes that are occurring today. It is by no means all of them.

Sept. 17, 2021 Microsoft Start, The Web: The planet is on a catastrophic path to reach 2.7 degrees Celsius according to a report on global emissions by the United Nations Framework Convention on Climate Change. The planet needs to reduce its emissions by 45% before 2030 in order to reach carbon neutral by 2050. But under the current rate of emissions, there will be a 16% increase in 2030 compared to 2010 levels according to the report. That would lead to the 2.7C degrees warming. Failure to meet carbon neutral will result in massive loss of life and livelihoods. It appears there is a high risk of failure. Carbon neutral is the point where we are reducing the same amount of CO_2 that we are emitting.

Oct. 2019, *National Geographic Magazine*, Species Extinction: "A recent intergovernmental report says that as many as one million species are already on their way to extinction. It's folly to think that we can throw away so much life, and not have it affect humanity in a profound way. Will we wake up and act or will we stare at our smartphones all the way down to disaster?"

July 15, 2019, *USA Today*, Alaska, Bethel: "Record high temperatures are believed to be the culprit behind salmon deaths in Western Alaska. Bethel based KYUK reports water temperatures on the Kuskokwim River broke 70 degrees last week, the highest on record."

10/5/21 *USA Today*, Stevens Village, Alaska: For the first time in memory King and Chum salmon migration on the Yukon River have dwindled to almost nothing and the state has closed salmon fishing there, even the subsistence harvest on which the Alaskan Natives relay on to fill freezers for their winter food supply. The Alaskan communities that dot the river are desperate. "Nobody has fish in their freezer right now. Nobody," said Giovanna Stevens, 38, a member of the Stevens Village tribe who grew up harvesting salmon. Those studying the catastrophe generally agree that climate change is responsible.

USA Today, 10/12/2021: Oregon Governor, Kate Brown is requesting Federal disaster relief for the commercial salmon fishing industry in her state.

Microsoft News-Internet. 6/9/2021, Canada launches $647 million strategy to stave off Pacific wild salmon collapse: "Many Pacific wild salmon are on the verge of collapse and we need to take bold action, ambitious action now if we are to reverse the trend and give them a fighting chance of survival," Fisheries Minister Bernadette Jorden said. Warming oceans due to climate change are altering the marine food web and resulting in warmer fresh water conditions pressuring salmon populations. Species such as the Chinook salmon on British Columbia's Frazer River are in steep decline and are struggling to return upstream to spawning grounds each year.

Sept. 30th, 2019, Arctic Melt: "The extent of the Arctic Sea ice reached its second lowest minimum on record on Sept. 18th, dropping to 1.6 million square miles. This effectually tied with 2007 and 2016 for that distinction. This year's minimum occurred four days later in summer then the average date between 1981 and 2010. All 13 lowest events on record have occurred during the past 13 years." A midsummer heat wave across parts of the North Atlantic caused enough of Greenland's ice cap to melt in 2021 in a single day, to submerge the entire state of Florida beneath 2 inches of water.

A new study out of Columbia University has determined that the summer Arctic Sea ice now covers half the space it did 40 years ago. Researchers say the sea ice will be "drastically thin" by 2050 endangering polar bears, walruses, seals, and other Arctic inhabitants. The summer sea ice is projected to be entirely gone by 2100. This will destroy the area's rich marine ecosystems.

April 13th, 2021, AOL Web Page: "Carbon dioxide and methane gas continue to rise in Earth's atmosphere, reaching their highest levels in the past 3.6 million years (as determined by ice cores taken in Antarctica). The last time that CO_2 was at its current level, global sea levels were 78 feet higher than they are today and the average global temperature was 7 degrees hotter. A study published in *Science Magazine* found that a massive ice shelf from Antarctic's Thwaites Glacier is even more unstable than previously thought due to warming waters melting the ice where it connects to land. A collapse of this single shelf would translate to a global sea level rise of up to 3 feet. Failure to slash the amount of added CO_2 into the atmosphere will make the extortionary heat, storms, wildfires, and ice melting in 2020 routine and could render significant portions of the earth uninhabitable."

Oct. 7th, 2020, IR: The average global temperature for September was 60.75 degrees Fahrenheit making it the hottest September ever recorded, the National Oceanic and Atmosphere Administration reported.

Sept. 5th, 2018, *USA Today*, Wilmington Delaware: Fisherman and scientist report that the state's coast is seeing more fish that are typically found further south due to warmer waters caused by climate change.

June 3, 2019, I.R., Climate Die Off: Change in the ocean's ecosystem off Alaska under global warming appears to be behind massive die-offs of seabirds in the Bering Sea. Researchers found that thousands of Tufted Puffers and a smaller number of Crested Anklets perished from starvation. Citizen scientist from Alaska's Pribilof Islands tribal communities joined with local officials and the University of Washington to document the birds' deaths and the environment in which they occurred. The report said that warmer weather and decreasing winter ice beginning in 2014 has led to decline in some of the marine species the seabirds feed on.

Oct. 2019, *National Geographic Magazine*, Fresh Water Species Extinction: Scientist believe that more than 20% of fresh water species are threatened or are already extinct, as dams constrain migration routes, habitats are made inhospitable by pollution runoff, and rising water temperature. Fresh water is less than 3% of all Earth's water but is home to almost half of all fish species.

Sept. 24th, 2019, *USA Today*, Heat Waves: Nine out of ten deadliest heat waves worldwide have occurred since 2000.

Oct. 10, 2019, Bird Extinction: A report by the National Audubon Society predicts that two-thirds of US birds face extinction by 2100 due to climate change if greenhouse emissions are not curbed: 389 out of 604 species in North America face extinction according to the Society.

Sept. 24, 2019, *USA Today*: Record-setting hot water in the Pacific Ocean will cause widespread bleaching and possible coral death. On the West Coast of Hawaii's big island, the ocean temperatures are about 3.5 degrees above normal for this time of year.

Sept. 20th, 2019, *USA Today*: How close to the tipping point of irreversible climate change do we need to come before people's infinite capacity to calmly watch their own demise is broken?

In just over the last twenty years, human-caused warming has intensified what would have been an ordinary dry period in the Southwest United States into a potential mega drought, the driest such period in 1200 years. Lake Powell and Lake Mead, the two largest man-made reservoirs in the US have been hit hard by persistent drought and the effect of climate change, warming, and drying in the last thirty years. Currently they are at levels not seen since they were built, both approaching less than 30% of capacity. Lake Mead has dwindled by almost 50 feet in just one year (2020). Forty million people depend on this source of water and the electricity generated by their turbines. They are also critical for supplying the water used by the huge agriculture regions in Arizona and the Imperial Valley in California that grow a large percentage of the produce we consume in the US.

The drought in the American West is not just a passing crisis; it is the future. The current drought covers an astounding 94% of the Western United States.

From the Web, Microsoft Start, 9/21/2021. California just had its warmest year on record.

The Web, Microsoft Solutions, 9/17/2021: Grasslands plants and their roots store about a third of the earth's carbon. They are one of nature's original climate-balancing solutions, removing CO_2 from the atmosphere and creating oxygen. Agriculture puts more CO_2 into the atmosphere then 150 million cars and accounts for more than 10% of the country's total emissions. Biodiversity is being destroyed by the relentless amount of corn and soybean farming. This results in the plowing of more lands releasing additional CO_2 into the atmosphere. Economics and politics are the main drivers of this due to two massive US Federal incentives, the ethanol mandate, which directs more than 100 million tons of corn to be produced as a gasoline additive along with crop insurance subsidies that protects growers from financial losses.

Food production and farming amount to 17.3 billion tons of CO_2 greenhouse gasses per year or 35% of all human-caused emissions. Fifty-seven percent of the food-related emissions were from animal-based foods, including crops grown to feed livestock. Beef is the largest contributor, responsible for 25% of all food emissions.

Scientists have warned us for many years that the earth and our way of life is in trouble unless we take the difficult steps to change and abandon our relentless push for unlimited growth. Over the last couple of years there has been increased recognition by the public that climate change is real and is a serious problem. Fortunately, there are attempts being made to start to correct our past errors and the lack of awareness of what is occurring. Unfortunately, these efforts are supported by a minority of our citizens, but hopefully that might be changing. The awareness should have started thirty years ago or earlier when the problem was recognized and ignored.

In a polling conducted in 2021 from Oct. 19–21, by Yahoo News/You Gov. found that only 48% of Americans favor cutting greenhouse gases in half by 2030 while more than a quarter (27%) are opposed. Only 50% of Americans surveyed view climate change as a threat, despite dire warnings from scientists for many years. More than 99% of scientific research reports on climate change confirms the crisis is being caused by human activity. However, 45% of Republicans, 29% of Independents and 4% of Democrats continue to deny the role that humans play in causing climate change according to the new polling data.

Many will remember former Vice President Al Gore, traveling the country and the world years ago showing graphs and lecturing about the rapid rise of CO_2 in the atmosphere and pleading for action. He was belittled, maligned, and called a fool; some fool. Even if we stopped all oil, coal, and gas production today, it is too late to arrest many of the existing effects of climate change. Reduce, reuse, recycle will not work anymore; it never has; extended long-term goals and pledges will be of little help. We cannot put drastic action aside and there is no modest solution. The bullet has to be bitten and that time is now. Is it too late to change? Will we continue down this path of the world's eventual destruction by political infighting, denials, and national and world stupidity?

Microsoft Start, The Web, 10/6/2021: The United Nations climate chief said that it is necessary to solve "the three planetary crises." Climate change, loss of biodiversity, and pollution and waste, if poverty in the world is going to be reduced. "Let me make this absolutely clear: loss of biodiversity means the loss of the planet's ability to sustain us. When you lose species and we are on the road to lose a million species out of the 7.8 million that are on the planet, and if we continue down the current track, the ecosystem cannot continue."

We must remember that since the last mass extinction, 65 million years ago, the earth had been reasonably stable. There has been ups and downs, a couple of severe ice ages, and huge heating events, but these occurred over sometimes millions of years of geological time periods.

What will be our period from the current time if we continue down this path? Five hundred years, a thousand years possibly more if we are lucky. But will our current way of life still exist?

9/27/2021, Microsoft Start, The Web: Scientists warn that by the year 2500 "large portions of the earth will be alien to humans due to climate change." That's just 400 years. Think how that compares to the millions of years it took to create the extinctions of the past when man was not on the scene.

9/17/2021, *The Washington Post* Web page: In the Klamath River watershed on the Oregon and California border, record low inflows are threating fish both in reservoirs and downstream rivers. The region is already seeing fish die-off from low stream levels and warm water temperatures.

Microsoft Start, The Web. 10/18/2021: Lake Tahoe is so low this year that its water is no longer flowing from the lake into the Truckee River preventing salmon from spawning in a major tributary this year, as reported by the *Los Angeles Times*.

USA Today, 12/13/2021, Minnesota. The state's lakes have lost nearly two weeks of ice over the last 50 years as climate change diminishes the length of winters.

I.R. 10/18/2021: South America's once mighty Parana River is now at its lowest level since 1941, causing thousands of acres of wetlands to dry up as well as threatening public water supplies and the livelihoods of fisherman and farmers. Experts say they don't know if this is part of a natural cycle or climate change. But there has been a three-year period of below-normal rainfall at the river's source in southern Brazil. Low water levels have also created a 50% drop in hydroelectric power generation plants along the Argentina-Paraguay border.

Desertification is the process that turns fertile farm land into barren land through interacting effects of human activity and climate extremes. In Spain about a fifth of all land is now at a high risk of desertification. This will increase worldwide as the earth warms and dries out and more extreme storms occur. Since the arrival of modern-day agriculture, humanity has degraded as much as a third of the world's farmland. In the United States, we are losing approximately 2% of our topsoil every year. Fertile soil is one of our basic life foundations, it takes a very long time to create even one inch of new topsoil. The Gobi Desert is a 500,000 square mile expanse stretching from Mongolia to Northwest China; it is expanding eastward. Every spring it creates dust that covers China's capital, Beijing, and also blows across the Pacific Ocean sometimes being recorded on the West Coast of the US.

The United Nations said recently that the latest round of the world's countries emission-reduction commitments still put the earth on a course for a "catastrophic" 2.7C of warming by the end of the century.

Global surface temperatures increases were 1.09C higher in the decade between 2011–2020 than between 1850–1900. The past five years have been the hottest on record since 1850 when recording began. A half of a degree Celsius does not sound like much, but a warming of just 2 degrees Celsius from the targeted 1.5C in 2050 could be the difference between life and death for millions of people. The recent rate of sea level rise has nearly tripled compared with 1901–1971, and the warming we have experienced to date has made changes to many of our planetary support systems that are irreversible on timescales of centuries and millennia.

The Web, 11/18/2021. Warmer Soils Store Less Carbon: Global warming will cause soils to release carbon into the atmosphere. In a scientific study of more than 9,000 soil samples from around the world, it was found that carbon storage "declines strongly as the average soil temperature increases." This is another example of "positive feedback" where global warming causes more carbon to be released. The soil types are important with low-clay soils losing three times as much carbon as fine-grained textured clays.

The researchers from the University Exeter and Stockholm University say their findings help to identify vulnerable stored carbon stocks. "Because there is more carbon stored in soils than there is in the atmosphere and all the trees on the planet combined, releasing even a small percentage could have significant impact on our climate," said Professor Lain Hartley of Exeter's College of Life and Environmental Scientists. It was found that carbon stores in coarse, textured soils at high latitudes are more likely to be the most vulnerable to climate change.

The availability of clean fresh water, or for that matter any fresh water in many parts of the world is already rapidly decreasing as the world heats up. The United Nations recently warned that 5 billion people throughout the world could have difficulty obtaining clean water by 2050. Only a small percent of the water on Earth is usable and available fresh water. The world's population continues to increase from today's almost seven billion to near the projected ten billion in 2050. Will there be basic resources available for these added billions of people?

The instabilities of climate change between countries have already arrived. The droughts caused by warming, less rainfall in certain areas of the world has put water and arable land at a premium, causing conflict between neighboring countries. Armed conflicts can occur when resources are under threat or contested followed by a shift in resources that changes caused by climate change. Conflict in Sudan and Syria over this have already occurred and mass migrations because by drought in Central America have caused large relocations. As the earth warms, these conditions will increase.

10/7/2021 Microsoft Start, The Web, The Conversation, Groundwater: Groundwater currently supplies drinking water to nearly half of the world's population and roughly 40% of water used in irrigation globally. Groundwater requires pumping and pumping requires energy. Many areas in the world where groundwater is needed to be used do not have available power. Over pumping can draw sea water and other pollutants into the aquifers and contaminate drinking supplies. This will increase as sea levels rise along low coastal areas.

The concentrations of gases in fossil groundwater (ancient water as old as 20,000 years or older) provide some of the most reliable estimates of temperatures on land during the last ice age. Such findings provide information into modern climates, including how sensitive Earth's average temperature is to carbon dioxide in the atmosphere. These methods support a recent study that found 3.4 degrees Celsius of warming with each doubling of the amount of CO_2. Most water stored underground has been there for decades and much for hundreds, thousands, and even millions of years. Ancient groundwater can take thousands of years to replenish naturally.

Daily Mail, The Web. 10/19/2021: Africa's glaciers will disappear by 2040 due to climate change, according to a report from the World Meteorological Organization (WMO). The report notes that the glaciers of Mount Kilimanjaro, Mount Kenya, and the Rwenzori Mountains are retreating at a rate faster than the global average due to the continent's warming at a dramatic rate. Kilimanjaro largest glacier has shrunk 70% between 2014 and 2020 and Rwenzori Mountains glaciers have lost up to 90% of their mass. The report warns that the melting of these glaciers will cause serious droughts and water shortages throughout eastern Africa. The rapid shrinkage of East Africa's glaciers indicates the threat of irreversible system change on Earth.

Microsoft, The Web 10/19/2021: A water crisis plagues tens of thousands in northeast Saria and Beirut, Lebanon. Ongoing water shortages are developing and creating a humanitarian crisis in these countries.

Microsoft, The Web: South Ghor, Jordan: Jordan is the second most water scarce country in the world, and water levels have been falling in recent years. Increased temperatures and lower rainfall plus rapid growth in population in the last decade due to the influx of refugees from neighboring Saria have seen water becoming increasing scarce and rapid groundwater depletion is occurring. The United Nations predicts that there will be a 40% shortfall worldwide in fresh water resources by 2030. What will it be in a hundred years?

The latest WMO report notes that the glaciers' loss is a grim reminder that Africa's 1.3 billion people remain extremely vulnerable. It's ironic that Africa's 54 countries are responsible for less than four percent of global greenhouse gas emissions.

Drought, Chennai, India: Extremely low rainfall in 2018 caused a devastating and historic drought that saw many of the reservoirs in the country's sixth largest city, dry up. The city's population of ten million people are suffering the consequences of the worst drought in seventy years.

Microsoft, The Web, *The Washington Post*, 10/31/21: Carbon dioxide added to the atmosphere takes centuries to dissipate. The recent atmospheric CO_2 measurements, the highest in 3 million years, signal that fossil fuel burning is hurtling us irreversibly into a much warmer future. CO_2 added to the atmosphere increases quickly but is only drawn down very slowly. Even if human emissions totally stopped tomorrow, what is there will stay there. The earth cannot begin to support enough living plants to hold the carbon from 60 million years of concentrated ancient vegetation contained in fossil fuels.

Can we count on technology to bail us out? New companies are starting up to address the challenge of removing CO_2 from the atmosphere, but the outlook for a near term miracle solution is not good. A new giant machine in Iceland does remove 4000 tons of CO_2 per year, but it would take 9 million of these machines all operated by non-carbon energy sources to remove all the carbon emissions that humans generate each year. And the process is very expensive costing between $600 to $800 dollars for each ton of carbon removed.

It's tempting to assume that global warming is a slow-moving crisis and that we can rely on technology to put the CO_2 genie back in the bottle. We must shake off this complacency. We have not invented a practical and safe method for removing more than a trivial fraction of the existing CO2 in our atmosphere and what will be added in the future; planting trees will not be the long-term answer.

Microsoft, The Web, 11/23/2021: Greenland's ice sheet has lost more than it gained for the 25th straight year. The ice sheet had a total loss of 166 gigatons of ice from September 2020 through August 2021. For the first time in recent human history, it rained on the ice sheet. The ice sheet also experienced the highest loss from calving and ocean melt since satellites began observing the loss in 1986. Scientists warn that the lost from calving and melting from ocean warming temperatures will not be compensated by cool summers and increase in snowfall.

The Web, 10/27/2021. Dying trees, Lebanon: Centuries-old cedar trees are at risk of disappearing due to global warming. Some of these trees are said to be 3000 years old and are mentioned in the Bible. They need a minimum amount of snow and rain, but global warming has meant they are subject to shorter and milder winters.

The Web, Pasterze, Austria. Pasterze Glacier: This glacier is losing around 16 feet of ice thickness every year. Many other glaciers in the region have shrunk dramatically and by the end of the century, they could all disappear.

The Web,11/7/2021: Kenya, drought has descended yet again in northern Kenya, the latest in a series of climate shocks rippling through the Horn of Africa. Kenya's government has declared a national disaster in 10 of its 47 counties. The United Nations says more than 2 million people are severely food insecure. People are trekking farther and farther in search of food and water. Observers warn conflicts could occur between communities.

The costal Northeast, from Maine to Delaware, is heating faster than most areas of the US due to a dramatic shift in the ocean atmospheric conditions over the North Atlantic. A study published in *Nature Climate Change* showed that not only are Northeastern winters getting warmer but that rapid summer warming is occurring along the Atlantic Coast. Researchers found that warming over the past century has exceed 2 degrees Celsius. That costal warming is nothing less than "exceptional" said lead author Ambarish Karmalkar, a professor at the University of Massachusetts, Amherst. "Some of the largest population centers in the US are suffering the greatest degree of warming," he said. The study was conducted with Columbia University climate scientist, Radley Horton.

Microsoft, The Web, 11/9/2021, Climate change is causing record warming in the Great Lakes: Lake Superior, for example is known to be frigid this time of year, but it was nearly 60 degrees in October and 51 degrees last week. Its normal average is about 45 degrees. All five of the Great Lakes have been one or two degrees above normal since October, according to the National Oceanic and Atmospheric Administration. These increases may not sound threatening, but Andrea Vander Woude, manager of NOAA's Great Lakes Environmental Research Laboratory Coast Watch program, told the *Detroit News*: "It could have a negative impact on many ecosystems such as fish, zooplankton, and the whole dynamics of small animals within the lakes."

Lake trout breed in the lakes around this time, but only if water temperatures are just right, Todd Wills, Lake Huron area fisheries research manager for the Michigan Department of Natural Resources said, "All fish have some sort of optimum temperature they survive at. When you get past that optimum temperature, even by a few degrees, things like their ability to grow, to spawn, and to survive can change. Even small changes in temperature for some species can really have a substantial effect."

A study this last September analyzed 60 lakes in the Northern Hemisphere and discovered water temperatures have steadily increased over the past 100 to 200 years. These water temperatures have increased more in the last 25 years than at any previous time. The lakes in the Northern Hemisphere are freezing about 11 days later and thawing seven days earlier. Sapna Sharnia, an associate professor at New York University told the *Washington Post*: "If we continue emitting greenhouse gasses at these rates, Lake Superior will not freeze after the 2060s."

United Nations - UN News, Global Perspective, The Web, 8/9/2021: Climate change is widespread, rapid, and intensifying and some trends are now irreversible according to the latest Intergovernmental Panel on Climate Change (IPCC) report. Human-induced climate change is changing the whole earth's climate system; in the atmosphere, in the oceans, ice floes, and on land. Many of these changes are unprecedented such as continued sea level rise are irreversible for thousands of years if ever. The report by 234 scientists from 66 countries states that human influence has warmed the climate faster than at any in the last 2000 years. Global mean sea level has risen faster since 1900, than in any preceding century in at least 3000 years.

The report reveals that human activities affect all major climate system components, with some responding over decades and others over centuries. These include increases in frequency and intensity of heat extremes; marine heat waves; heavy precipitation; droughts in some regions; more intense tropical cyclones; reduction in Arctic Sea ice, snow cover; and increased permafrost melting. The scientists also caution that possible ice sheet collapse or abrupt ocean circulation changes cannot be ruled out.

One important thing everyone must come to understand and remember is that what the scientists have been telling us about the pending extreme weather events for years are now occurring before our very eyes and sometimes even in our front yards. We should pay very close attention to what they are saying about the impending climate warming in the future. With climate change increasing, nobody, including us, is left off the endangered species list.

Vanishing glaciers: Canadian scientists say the massive glaciers that blanket parts of the western Yukon are shrinking much faster than would be expected under global warming. The glacier retreat has cut off critical water supplies to Kluane Lake causing the level of the UNESCO World Heritage Site to drop more than 6 feet. This has stranded thousands of fish from their traditional spawning grounds. "The region is one of the hot spots for warming we've come to realize over the last 15 years," said David Hik of Simon Frazer University. "The magnitude of change is dramatic."

Yahoo News, The Web, 11/18/2021: The weather events on the West Coast of Canada have given us a glimpse of our perilous environmental future. In June, British Columbia was setting under a highly irregular "heat dome" that drove temperatures to record heights. Fires, smoke, and life-threatening heat were especially bad, with the town of Lytton recording 121 degrees Fahrenheit and ending with the town being completely consumed by fire.

Just a few months later, an "atmospheric river" has brought widespread storms with continual heavy rains, road washouts, and mudslides. The Port of Vancouver and other marine terminals have been cut off from the rest of Canada by road and rail closures. A government official said it could take several weeks or months to repair the major highways and get them open again because the flooding has been so widespread. The western province of British Columbia has been declared a state of emergency, entire towns are under water, and 18,000 people have been stranded; water systems are polluted, gas lines severed, and thousands of cattle killed. It's just the latest disturbing evidence of what awaits the world over the coming years and decades.

USA Today, 9/30/2021, Phoenix and other fast-warming cities: The average temperature in Phoenix has increased 4.35 degrees since 1970, according to a 2019 Climate Control report. Cities including Burlington, Vermont; Chattanooga, Tennessee, and Helena, Montana are right behind Phoenix as members in Climate Centers top 10 fastest warming cities list, experiencing temperature rises of more than 4 degrees. In 2020 Phoenix had the hottest driest summer on record with 53 days of temperatures equal to or exceeding 110 degrees. It has been suggested that the city plants thousands of trees to help mitigate the problem, but trees require water and time to grow and the city is already stressed for adequate water supplies that it receives primarily from the Colorado River and Lake Mead.

Excerpts From the *USA Today* Special Report, "Downpour." 12/3/2021: There has been a stunning shift in the way rain and snow fall across the country and how that affects our environment, our infrastructure, and our lives. It is true that extreme weather events do occur naturally, but the frequency and intensity of what is now occurring in our country and around the world make it hard to ignore their obvious connection with the change in the climate.

Now larger concentrations of dangerous rainfall and severe droughts are growing. Scientists tell us as more greenhouse gases accumulate in the atmosphere, they cause the earth to warm. The warming intensifies how water in the atmosphere circulates. The excess heat causes increased evaporation, mostly from the oceans, drawing more water into the air where it can produce more relentless storms. By changing the weather patterns, this can produce extreme heat, droughts, and fires in the West and persistently increase the amount of rain in the Eastern part of the country, both occurring in the same time periods. Heat changes how moisture moves across the country. It alters the flow of the jet stream, extends droughts by increasing evaporation from the land, drawing moisture from trees and plants, thereby enabling the intensified frequency and severity of wild fires.

At the same time, more rain is falling in the East: In Tennessee in August 2021 in the small city of McEwen, 12 inches of rain fell in just seven hours. The total rain for the storm; 17 inches that broke the state's rainfall record and triggered deadly flooding.

While in the West, more record-breaking wildfires were occurring. All but two of California's 20 largest wildfires have occurred since 2003. Oregon had a record fire season in 2021 with approximately 2200 fires that burned 1.1 million acres and destroyed 4000 homes. Then in late October an atmospheric river of moisture dropped from 3 to 13 inches of rain across California, Oregon, Washington, and Nevada causing widespread flooding in many areas. Scientists state that two things appear to be true: "Everyone is getting warmer and everyone is seeing or will experience soon, more intense precipitation and drought events."

The investigation by *USA News* used 126 years of monthly data from the National Oceanic and Atmospheric Administration to study the annual precipitation at 344 climate-monitoring locations around the country. The purpose of the study was to measure the frequency of extreme weather events across the US from 1951–2020.

They found that more than half of the nation's 344 measuring sites had their wettest periods on record since 2018. East of the Rockies, more rain fell with greater intensity and in the West, people were waiting longer to see any rain at all. At some point over the last three years, 27 eastern states had their greatest 30-year precipitation average since record-keeping started in 1895. A dozen states saw five of their wettest years in history occur over the past two decades. Michigan saw six of its wettest 10 years on record over the past 13 years. In June 2021, at least 136 daily rainfall records were set across five states bordering the Mississippi River. In the West, over the same time period eight states had at least three record-dry years. That is double what is normal based on historical records. "People talk about the future effects of climate change, but the reality is climate change is here now and its affecting most of us," stated Michael Mann, a climatologist at Penn State University. These persistent weather events are all interconnected and are influencing how climate change is creating modifications around the country.

The point of all this work is to help people understand the impact of climate change now in their daily lives. These extreme events are not a onetime thing, they are all parts of the same design. "There is a lot that all of us need to do to wrap our brains around the new reality we are living in."

> "Democracy destroys itself because it abuses its right to freedom and equality. Because it teaches its citizens to consider audacity as a right, lawlessness as a freedom, abrasive speech as equality, and anarchy as progress."
> – Isocrates: 436–338 BC

SPECIES

USA Today, 10//19/2021, Monarch butterflies: The monarch butterflies in California have declined 99% in the last three decades. More than 1.2 million were reported in 1997, a recent survey in 2020 only 1,900 were found. These are the western butterflies that spend the winter in California and Oregon on the west side of the Rocky Mountains. The eastern monarchs that migrate to Mexico in winter and stay east of the Rockies, have declined 80%. Housing expansion, drought, and wildfires have depleted their habitat, and pesticides and herbicides have brought the monarch to the brink of extinction. Like all ecosystems' collapse, the problem is not just one thing but many things over long time periods that lead to destruction.

USA Today, Portland Maine. Maines's puffins: The birds suffered one of the worst years for reproduction in decades this summer as warmer oceans reduced the availability of the small fish they eat. There are about 1500 breeding pairs in the state that rely on fish such as herring and sand lances to feed their young. Only about a quarter of the birds this summer were able to raise chicks. About two-thirds are successful in a normal year.

Reuters, The Web, 10/19/2021: French beekeepers expect the worst harvest in decades due to climate change. Cold and wet weather has prevented bees from producing honey. The Beekeepers Association (UNAF) said based on reports received from regional associations the expected harvest to be about one third of the 2020 harvest. "This will be the worst harvest in the history of our organization, the worst in 50 years," UNAF present told Reuters. He said future bad weather and changing climate will have a lasting impact on honey production.

Microsoft, The Web, Amaze Laboratories, 10/18/2021: Because of warming oceans, plankton are beginning to migrate and that could have catastrophic consequences. Plankton are the second most numerous species in the world after bacteria. New evidence suggests that a movement towards the poles will occur if ocean temperatures reach 77 degrees Fahrenheit. Plankton are the major oxygen producers in the ocean; they are absolutely necessary in the food chain; without them most every marine species would parish.

Microsoft, The Web, 10/31/2021: Turkeys Lake Tuz has been the breeding grounds for Flamingoes for centuries; they migrate there each year to feed on the shallow lake's algae. Rapidly changing climate and unsustainable agriculture practices have led to drought that killed thousands of flamingoes this summer. Lake Tuz is Turkey's second largest lake at 643 square miles. It totally dried up this year due to the ever-warming climate and extensive water use for agriculture.

Turkey's largest lake, Lake Van lost so much water that fishing boats were unable to dock. Climate scientist say these two examples reflect the serious conditions stemming from lack of water in other bodies of water across the Mediterranean basin caused by drought and a land degradation process known as desertification, causing farmland to turn into desert. The area's groundwater supplies have declined because of over pumping. There are about 120,000 unlicensed wells in the region that are pumping water as if it will last forever.

The Web, 11/5/2021. Drought and over pumping closed Morocco river link to the sea: The Moulouya River, one of the longest rivers in North Africa and vital for people and farmers in the area no longer flows into the sea due to over pumping of groundwater and the changing climate. As the fresh water recedes, salty seawater is encroaching into the fresh groundwater.

Associated Press, The Web, 9/4/2021. International Union of Conservation of Nature: Thirty seven percent of the ocean's rays and sharks are considered in danger of extinction as of 2021, up from 33% seven years ago due to overfishing, a loss of habitat and climate change. Total shark populations have declined 71% since 1970.

Fisheries: Large areas of the North Sea and the Atlantic have been overfished. Halibut numbers were once so large off the northeast coast of North America that a single fishing boat could land 20,000lbs. in a single day. Now halibut are almost extinct off the northeast coast. The cod fishery is another example. The Georges Banks off Massachusetts and the Grand Banks off Newfoundland for centuries were so dense with cod, some weighing over a hundred pounds, they were thought to be inexhaustible. By 1960 the numbers of spawning cod in the North Atlantic had fallen to 1.6 million tons. By 1990 this had shrunk to 22,000 tons. It was feared that the cod may have been lost forever. In 1992 cod fishing was terminated.

Quieter Spring, I.R., 11/8/2021: The natural soundscape across much of North America and Europe appears to have become quieter and less diverse over the past 25 years, in which researchers say bird numbers have plummeted. Simon Butler of Britain's University of East Anglia analyzed sound clips with acoustic modeling of more than a thousand bird species that were recorded in Europe and North America between 1996 and 2018. He and his colleagues found there was a sharp decline in both diversity and intensity of birdsong, mirroring the loss of bird populations during the study period. It has been documented that the calls and other sounds made by the winged creatures can have a positive effect on human well-being and connect us with the natural world. "All bird songs are love songs."

I.R., 9/30/2021: The present administration said it will reinstate rules terminated by the last president that holds companies responsible for bird kills. The move comes as North American bird numbers have plummeted drastically in the last few decades. The administration got immediate pushback from the oil industry, which had to pay an $100 million settlement for their killing of about 100,000 birds. The Independent Petroleum Company of America said this action would "harm business." This law had been in effect for a century before it was cancelled. Hundreds of millions of birds are killed by collisions with glass buildings, power lines, poisoned, and killed in oil company oil pits. Almost three billion birds have been lost in the last 50 years. More than 1000 bird species are covered with the new regulations, some close to extinction.

I.R., 8/20/2019, Anchorage Alaska: "Dead salmon have shown up in river systems throughout the state this summer and mortalities are likely linked to warm or low water levels," says Sam Rabeing, director of commercial fisheries for Alaska Department of Fish and Game.

USA Today, 7/14/2021, Stuart, Florida: More than a thousand manatees have died this year due to starvation, because of the loss of the seagrass beds they feed on, caused by warmer water and pollution. Algae blooms fed by pollution were the main cause for destroying thousands of acres of seagrass in the Indian River Lagoon, a major manatee feeding area.

FINANCIAL

The severe weather-related storms that the world is experiencing today, and the massive loss of homes and other properties are increasing. How long can society continue to afford to pay for these horrendous increasing losses as climate change becomes more intense, as it will, and the storms more severe? Will Mother Nature bankrupt us? More important, how long can humanity continue to cope with the trauma of destructive storms and flooding, one after another? How many times can you repair and rebuild your homes and businesses before it gets overwhelming?

When we look at what has happened in the past, we can better understand what the future will bring. According to the US Energy Department, in the 1980s the US spent an average of $13 billion per year cleaning up after extreme weather events. In the 1990s we spent $27 billion per year. That figure rose to $51 billion by the 2000s. Now, over the last three years, these costs increased again to $152 billion per year. Most recently the US spent $130 billion to clean up a single winter storm in Texas. Today it is estimated that it will cost the US $100 billion to $150 billion for the latest destructive hurricane, Ida. Many people today cannot get flood insurance and if they can, it is becoming very expensive as the losses continue to surge. How do you live in an area with these conditions and without insurance? You don't, you move., you immigrate and sometimes on a massive scale.

Washington: The Biden administration is taking steps to address the economic risk from climate change issuing a 40-page report on a plan to protect the insurance, financial, and housing markets and the savings of American families. The report lays out steps that could potentially alter the mortgage process, stock market disclosures, retirement plans, federal procurement, and government budgeting. It calls on the government to analyze how the world's largest economy could be affected by extreme heat, flooding, storms, wildfires, and the broader adjustments to address climate change. Studies are fine if they lead to rapid action that produce meaningful results, otherwise we again are just spinning our wheels as the world tans.

Reuters, The Web, 11/11/2021. US flood insurance rates to rise for 77% of policyholders: The new premiums will be based on a property's value, risk of flooding and other factors rather than simply on a home's elevation. Premiums for 3.3 million policies holders will see monthly payments rise $10 or more. As of April, FEMA flood insurance program provided $1.3 trillion dollars in coverage and has been losing money.

The extreme weather events the country and the world are experiencing today are not a one-time deal. The climate crisis isn't a future problem; it's here today with severe and frequent hurricanes, tornados, dangerous heavy rainfall and flooding, massive wildfires, and the loss of fresh water and more tragic the loss of lives. It is a threat to civilizations as we know it, and will get worse.

The massive loss of forest, homes, and other properties in the West due to fires and flooding will continue to add to these costs. The insurance industry has 4.7 trillion dollars invested in the financial markets at the end of 2020 according to the Treasury Department as posted in the Federal Register. How long can these companies, the communities and the people that are directly affected by these tragedies cover the increasing billions of dollars of losses in the future before they collapse and become financially extinct? The future is not tomorrow; it's ten thousand tomorrows.

Microsoft, The Web,10/23/2021: Humans and climate change have transformed 10 of the world's most highly protected forests into net emitters of carbon over the last 20 years. Wide swaths of the Amazon Forest have been clear cut or burned to clear land for cattle or agriculture, critically reducing the forest ability to absorb carbon.

Fox Business, 10/19/2021: It has been reported that America will be faced with a demand for a large amount of money by the developing countries at the coming climate conference at Glasgow, Scotland.

John Kerry, the US climate envoy at a meeting with representatives of poor countries, was presented with a demand for $750 billion dollars every year to help them quit using fossil fuels. Is there any possibility of the US voters agreeing to send almost a trillion dollars a year overseas to these poor countries? What happens if we don't, will they continue their uncontrolled use of fossil fuels?

A recent Bank of America Global Research report (BAG) found that the consequences of climate change will be dire and extreme. "This is the last decade to act," the authors wrote. Absolute water scarcity is likely for 1.8 billion people, 100 million face poverty and 800 million are at risk of rising sea levels by 2025. Migration caused by climate could reach 143 million from poorer countries driven by warmer weather and scarce water.

The cost to reduce carbon releases to sustainable levels could reach 5 trillion dollars a year according to the report. It is the annual amount that will be the average for the next 30 years. A massive number of $150 trillion dollars, said Hain Israel, Director of Research at Bank of America/Merrill Lynch. This number is almost twice the total global GDP in 2019. This cost is for the transition of emitting industries into cleaner industries.

Who in their right mind thinks this is going to be possible without destroying the world's economy? But yet, if the release of additional vast amounts of carbon into the atmosphere continue, these costs would appear to be a pittance in comparison to the damage and hurt the warming world will suffer. Again, the dilemma, we can't afford these tremendous transition costs yet, we cannot afford not to afford them, so where does that leave the planet?

Regardless of the report's projections, the high costs today for the natural disasters and droughts are already occurring and within a few decades the total costs will be astronomical as warming continues, migrations increase, and industrial upheaval accelerates. The warming climate will worsen every existing service, from water and sewage treatment, mass transit, food distribution, and health care while eroding the wealth of millions of people.

ENERGY

> The scientists say that 85% of matter is dark matter and they don't even know what that is. Well, if it is the most abundant thing in the universe, it has to be made of stupidity.
>
> – Dilbert cartoon

Despite the need to make significant reductions to greenhouse gas emissions, many producing countries are actually projecting an average increase in fossil fuel production of 2% annually until 2050. We must today without delay realize that future development and use of fossil fuels is no longer suitable for the planet. The government must stop allowing development of fossil fuels in the ocean by banning the sale of new off-shore leases. There should be no more government handout to the oil industry. There has been $7.6 billion dollars per year of taxpayer's money from 2017 to 2019 spent supporting the oil and gas industry through tax breaks, direct payments of taxpayers' dollars and public finance. This has got to stop. We need a carbon tax on all carbon emissions to incentivize them to invest in renewable energy by putting a price on emissions.

Unfortunately, oil will still be required in large quantities. We cannot lubricate our industrial complex with the sun and wind. Diesel will still be necessary, there are trains and ships and diesel trucks to run. Kerosene for aviation fuel will be required on a large scale. Unfortunately, there is no free lunch. The world has reached another real dilemma: How do we continue to control the heating of our planet and maintain a stable economic environment?

And then this question arises: How much longer will these non-renewable sources of energy, oil, and gas, last? We have been burning them at a prodigious rate; two, three, five hundred years? Very short time spans if we expect to still be around.

Another critical necessity for the country's industry is rare earth minerals. They are absolutely necessary for today's production of viewing screens, such as cell phones, iPad screens, TVs, and GPS devices in the newer automobile models. Without them certain colors are not possible. Some of their known reserves are less than one hundred years.

Most all of the supply and production of these minerals comes from China. We import nearly 100% of them. They are also used in high performance optics and lasers, the most powerful magnets and super conductors. They are also used in exotic light sources, special type glasses, electrodes, coloring in ceramics and glass radiology equipment, cell phones, and iPads. When they become truly rare, we will lose a lot of our toys.

Will we be able to diversify our economies away from major use of coal, oil, and gas in time to ward off a future complete shutdown of the planet? In just a hundred years, it is projected that the average global temperature, given the present rate of growth, is expected to rise as much as 7 degrees Fahrenheit. If that is allowed to occur, much of Earth's surface will be a frying pan and uninhabitable. Just 100 years. One thing should be very clear, any fossil fuel investment made today will have a substantial loss as the climate continues to warm.

Fossil fuels account for more than 80% of global energy use and they also are essential for the making of thousands of other products. Most all plastics are manufactured using fossil fuels. Will the rush for profits and political pressures override the need for immediate drastic action? How will the earth change course in time and will we be able to survive without our pickup trucks, busses, trains, aircraft, pleasure craft, seagoing commercial transport, cruise liners, plastics, and thousands of other uses and products that use fossil fuels, that we rely on today? We have been caught in a serious predicament of our own making. We are dammed if we continue the path we are on and dammed if we don't.

A study published in the *Journal of Nature* found that nearly 60% of the planet's unused oil and natural gas and 90% of its coal reserves should not be developed and should stay in the ground until 2050 if we are going to have any chance of reaching carbon natural by then, when we will hopefully be removing the same amount of CO_2 as we are sending into the atmosphere. What is the chance of this happening?

Sept.27, 2021, Microsoft Start, The Web: China manufactures the majority of the solar panels produced around the world. A large amount of electricity is used in the manufacturing process. In China, that electricity overwhelmingly comes from coal-burning power plants. This generates twice as much carbon dioxide into the atmosphere than the equivalent panels made elsewhere. The solar industry, when it depends on the cheaper panels manufactured by Chinese coal seriously defeats their benefits.

There have been expensive attempts in the past to develop "clean coal." There is no such thing we have belatedly learned. Billions of dollars have been spent to develop clean coal and nothing has come of it. The demolition (blown up) of the country's largest plant devoted to that effort was just completed. It was 2.4 billion dollars in debt after years of propaganda as to how successful the effort was.

I.R., Solar Meltdown, 10 /18/2021: The earth's reliance on electronics could make the planet vulnerable to a global internet meltdown should a solar storm as powerful as the one that occurred in the pre–hi-tech year of 1859 by knocking out our massive electronic technology. The Carring event of Sept 1–2, 1859, caused serious damage to telegraph systems of that day. Researcher, Sangeetha Jyothi said that while local and regional fiber networks wouldn't be badly affected by such a large-scale solar storm, she is concerned about the repeaters used to connect the world's vast undersea cable system. Earlier studies have warned that other technology, especially orbiting satellites, could be fried by an intense storm.

MIGRATION

10/7/2021 Microsoft Start, Reuters.: The vicious cycle of the depletion of natural resources tied to violent conflict may have gone past the point of no return in parts of the world and is likely to increase due to climate change.

Food insecurity, lack of water, and the impact of natural disasters, combined with high population growth are creating conflicts and displacing people. The Institute for Economics and Peace used data from the United Nations to predict the countries and regions most at risk. The report identified 30 hotspot countries around the world, as facing the most risks and conflicts. The report is based on criteria relating to scarcity of resources, disasters, including floods droughts, and rising temperatures.

It estimated by the World Bank (2018) that 140 million people might be displaced from Africa, South, and central Asia, and Central and South America, Eastern Europe, and the Pacific due to fresh water shortages, agriculture failures, decreased crop yields, rising sea levels, flooding, and political upheavals. It's already happening in some parts of the world. This insecurity creates hazards of conflicts, famine, and deaths for millions of peoples. If emissions are not controlled, that figure could balloon to 216 million people moving somewhere within their own countries and across six regions of the world. Sub-Saharan Africa would see the most movement with up to 86 million climate migrants moving due to desertification, fragile coastlines, and severe fresh water scarcity.

The health of the world will also be affected as people move spreading disease. More than 200 of the world's leading health journals released a statement that said climate change is the greatest threat to public health. *The Lancet*; *British Medical Journal*; the *New England Journal of Medicine*; the *Medical Journal of Australia*, and others have stated: "Health is already being harmed by global temperature increases and the destruction of the natural world." The consensus of these journals agrees. "If we continue at the present levels, the loss of biodiversity risk and the harm to health will be impossible to reverse."

I.R. Bird Migrations, 11/1/2021: Climate change appears to causing many migratory birds to spend between 50 and 60 fewer days in their historic African wintering homes, and new research says some species may stop migrating southwards from Europe entirely. Scientists from Britain's Durham University say records from 1964 to 2019 reveal that some species are arriving at their winter grounds later in autumn and departing earlier in the spring. A reduction in the time the birds spend in Africa could have implications, such as insect consumption, seed dispersal, and pollination.

Migrations within the United States will also occur on a massive scale as the change in the climate causes rising sea levels, floods, drought, fires, and fresh water availability. It will seriously increase political and economic instability in the US. Our country is more inclined to spend resources to repair the damage than to finance the steps necessary to prevent it. Unfortunately, the moment to address the problem is long past due. We are playing catch-up and the ballgame is in the late innings.

Climate Famine, *Independent Record*: The deepening food crisis affecting Madagascar after five years of extreme weather events is being called the first climate-induced famine by the UN's World Food Program (WFP). About 1.3 million people there are suffering from acute hunger, with 30,000 in the grip of famine due to loss of crops and livestock. Some are eating cactus leaves and insects in order to survive. WFP Deputy Country Director in Madagascar Aduino Mangoni said huge numbers have moved to urban centers in search of help. He added that while famines elsewhere have mainly been driven by conflict, "This is basically the only, maybe the first climate-change famine on earth."

Microsoft, The Web, 11/13/2021: A United Nations agency's recent report revealed that a rising number of people worldwide are fleeing violence, insecurity, and water shortages and the effects of climate change with over 84 million people relocating within and beyond their own home countries during the first half of this year.

HEALTH

The fierce wildfires that have occurred over the western United States in the last few years have spread smoke over hundreds of square miles continue to pose serious health problems for millions of people. This is of concern because the microscopic particles in wildfire smoke carried by the wind can penetrate deep into people's lungs and travel in the bloodstream. One study linked wildfire smoke exposure to a two-fold increase in the rate of asthma and a 40% rise in strokes and heart attacks. Other studies have tied smoke to hospital admissions and premature deaths.

Smoke and ash from wildfires can be release in silt runoff from burned areas that contain parasites, bacteria, and other containments. The cost to communities to filter and clean such water can be very expensive. Sediment flows from burned areas after a fire can sometimes last for long periods after the fire.

IR, Climate Related Health Problems, 10/2/2021: Health problems tied to climate change are getting worse, according to two reports published Wednesday. The annual report commissioned by the medical journal *Lancet* tracked 44 global health indicators connected to climate change, including heat deaths, infectious diseases, and hunger. All of them are getting worse said *Lancet* communications project director Marina Romanello, a biochemist. Rising temperatures are having consequences said University of Washington director Krisitie Ebi, the report's coauthor. In the US, heat, fire, and drought have caused the biggest problems. The report said an unpresented heat wave in the Pacific Northwest this summer could not have happened without human-caused climate change.

Safe vaccines have been free and available in this country for over a year yet there are still over 60 million Americans that have not been or refused to be vaccinated. How can anyone refuse a known, proven safe treatment that could save their lives? The death toll in this country rose from 600,000 to 700,000 in just three and a half months. Florida and Texas accounted for 30% of the deaths since the 700 thousand sad milestone was reached. Why? It has been determined that 70 thousand of the 100 thousand deaths were people who were un-vaccinated. If those two states and the rest of the country had any commonsense leadership and been more concerned and taken measures to insist that people get vaccinated rather than playing politics with people's lives, 90% of those deaths could have been prevented since mid-June. It was a self-extinction pandemic of the un-vaccinated caused by a total lack of leadership and political brainwashing that killed seventy thousand Americans. Each one of those who adamantly refused to protect themselves or others around them by being vaccinated essentially committed unintended personal suicide and that's the worst form of extinction. And if they infected innocent people who also lost their lives, unintended manslaughter, there is no other way to call it.

> "Man must obtain his knowledge and chose his actions by the process of thinking, which nature will not force him to perform. Man has the power to act as his own destroyer and that is the way he has acted throughout most of history."
> – Ann Rand

PLASTICS AND POLLUTION

Plastics are primarily made from fossil fuels in an energy intensive process that emits greenhouse gases. Their demand and increased production have rapidly risen between 2015 and 2020 and were responsible for emitting 56 billion megatons of CO_2. This amounts to between 10 to 13 percent of the total global emissions into the atmosphere. So, it is more than just gas-burning cars that has to be addressed.

It is estimated that by 2019, the oceans contained 180 million tons of plastic and that about 8 million tons are added each year. We live in a world where the oceans cover 71 percent of the earth's surface. It is vital for us, producing more oxygen than the largest rain forest and it stores 50 times more carbon than what's in our atmosphere. It contains over 700,000 individual species.

It's not possible to know exactly the total amount of plastics in the ocean and the estimates made by scientific studies are constantly being updated but there is no doubt that the amount is very large. According to the United Nations study around 300 million tons of plastic waste is produced globally each year, about 9% is recycled, 12% is incinerated and the rest ends up in landfills or spread over the earth or in the oceans. But this we do know, a plastic trash-filled area between Hawaii and California is the largest accumulation of ocean plastic in the world; called the Great Pacific Garbage Patch, it has been estimated to contain more than 1.8 trillion pieces of plastic.

Microplastics are very small particles of plastic that are the result of the disintegration of larger pieces that occur over time periods depending on their chemical makeup and exposure to sunlight, sometimes taking many years.

Fish and Marine life Contaminated with Plastics: One study found that over 70% of deep-sea fish caught in the North Atlantic Ocean had ingested plastic, this included cod and haddock. The amount they consumed depended on the species and the area in the ocean where they live. If things continue, the quantity of plastics (by weight) in the ocean in 2050 will equal the weight of all the fish.

It is estimated that 90% of all seabirds ingest plastic and by 2050 that may rise to 99%. Around one million seabirds die each year from getting tangled up in or eating plastic.

Microplastics have been found in about 90% of commercial sea salt. Fortunately, most plastic is concentrated in fish stomachs that is not consumed by humans. The on-going question is how much of this plastic can be concentrated in other parts of the fish. This has not been determined.

Plastic pollution is having a devastating impact on the ocean's biodiversity. Scientific studies have shown that stark changes are already occurring from both plastic pollution and climate change that affect marine organisms. This is disrupting the oceans' ecosystems and food sources from the smallest sea life to the largest whales. Over decades or even centuries plastic breaks down into tiny particles that can contaminate our food, air, and water. They can accumulate in our bodies causing chronic inflammation and other ills.

Plastic Resistance, Independent Record, 12/13/2021: Broken down microplastics are providing homes for microbes and chemical contaminants and researchers say they also attract free-floating genetic material that can deliver antibiotic resistance to bacteria. An international team found that microplastics broken down by the sun's ultraviolent light made perfect homes for antibiotic-resistant microbes that can be passed on to people.

In a report published in the *Journal of Hazardous Materials*, scientists say enhanced dissemination of antibiotic resistance is an overlooked potential impact of microplastics pollution.

The United States alone in 2016, generated 46.3 million tons of plastic. That amounts to 287 pounds per person in just one year. Surely that has increased since then. It is estimated that plastic use will more than double worldwide by the year 2050. Is it possible that we can drastically reduce its use before then, and if not, where will all the plastics go?

An example as to the inclusion of plastics into our environment; Sampling Finds Plastic Pollution in Montana's Fresh Water: Plastic pollution was found in more than half of the 50 water samples taken around the state. The goal of the study was to examine the presence and types of microplastics near fishing access sites. Ten quarts of water were taken at each site: all jars were labeled and recorded with samplings numbered, site description and date. The jars were then sent to the lab for processing. Identified microplastics were categorized into four types.

1. Fibers from synthetic fabrics and filaments such as fishing lines and bailing twine.
2. Fragments from rigid plastic, including polystyrene and clear plastic containers.
3. Films from plastic bags and food wrappers.
4. Microbeads from older personal care products.

Of the 50 sites tested, 33 (66%) contained one or more types of plastic. That's happening today. What will be the results in 100 years?

Air Pollution: Levels of particulate matter today in California, Oregon, Nevada, Idaho, and Washington are more than twice the recommend safe limits mostly caused by wildfire smoke. Particulate matter is a mix of microscopic solids and liquid droplets that are 2.5 micrometers in diameter, or roughly one-thirtieth the width of a human hair. Commonly found in wildfire smoke and vehicle exhaust, especially diesel exhaust, they have been connected to respiratory-related hospital admissions and increased mortality. When you inhale these particles, they are able to penetrate deeper into your respiratory system and once these particles enter the lungs, they also can cross over into the bloodstream and even the organs.

IR, 9/13/2021, Pollution Kills: A new report highlights how air pollution, mainly from coal, is impacting life expectancy far greater than diseases such as tuberculosis and HIV/AIDS, and even behavior such as smoking cigarettes. The Asir Quality Life Institute reveals that unless particulate pollution is reduced to meet World Health Organization guidelines, the average person will lose about 2.2 years of his or her life. Even though China has slashed its air pollution, dirty air is still cutting about 2.6 years off its life spans. India has made no such efforts, and its citizens lose 5.9 years off their lives, especially in highly polluted areas in the north of the country.

Microsoft, The Web, Concrete, 10/19/2021: If concrete were a country, it would be the third largest emitter of greenhouse gases on Earth, just behind the US and China. How can this material, essential for global housing construction and infrastructure be made less damaging? Cement is the most utilized material on earth, it is being made at a rate of some 150 tons a second according to the Global Cement and Concrete Association (GCCA). About 14 billion cubic meters of concrete is cast each year. In order to produce one ton of cement, the process of making cement produces one ton of CO_2. The concrete industry has said it wants to be carbon neutral by 2050. How?

INFRASTRUCTURE

There has been an 134% increase in flood disasters since 2000 while the number and duration of droughts have grown by 29%. It is not only climate change; population growth and development play a large role in the ever-increasing disruptions occurring on the planet.

How many years will it take for Lake Powell and Lake Mead to be silted in? A hundred, two hundred, or maybe five hundred years or longer, but it will happen. Look at the Grand Canyon; at one time it was a river running across a high desert. In a short period of geological time, it has gradually continued to cut its way deeper and deeper through ancient ocean sediments creating the majestic panorama we view today. It's not an old canyon, ten million years or so, and it's not done growing.

But where did all that soil go as it was slowly washed down, eroded, and carried as sediment by the river? We are farming it today. As it was carried down to lower and more level elevations, the river spread out and deposited billions of tons of fertile soil layer on layer as the river changed courses through the millilumens. Vast quantiles were also carried to the Gulf of California where it was dispersed by the large tidal boors created at the upper end of the Gulf by tidal action. The immense southern farmlands of Arizona, California, and Mexico that are so rich and productive and that we depend on for most of our produce, are the result.

But the river still runs and the erosion and silting continue to flow, only now the silt's travel has been slowed by the dams. It no longer can be dispersed; it is concentrated and has nowhere to go except to grow deeper and deeper until there is no more room. Unless someway is found to remove the large quantities of silt in the deep lakes, two majestic waterfalls will occur flowing over the dams. It may not happen for a thousand years or more, but it will happen. Today the silt is not the concern, both of the lakes impounded behind these dams are at record lows at thirty percent of capacity and in a serious state for their ability to provide water for farmland irrigation and drinking water for millions of people.

The majority of the structures we see today, our massive concrete dams, mega high-rise buildings, oil pipelines and highways will be our pyramids in four thousand years. Do we really believe that an oil pipeline buried in corrosive soil or salt water will last a hundred, two hundred years without failing and destroying a segment of the environment? None of our great structures will survive the ravages of time any better than the ancient Egyptians' monumental efforts, and if current trends continue, there won't be many tourists.

Great nations and great empires are like human beings. They are born, they grow, they mature, they decline, and then they die. Where are we today in that cycle, where are the empires of the past, how did they die, and what of those of the future? Just four thousand years. How does that compare to the time of the dinosaurs who were around for 150 million years?

10/15/2021 Microsoft Start, the Web, Source: Environmental Defense Fund (EDF) and McGill University. Abandoned Wells: Oil and gas wells that have been drilled and then abandoned; an analysis done by the EDF found that there were 81,203 documented wells across the country that were drilled and then improperly abandoned by oil and gas companies. Each of these orphan wells is a major climate problem that can release methane gas. The wells are in most all of the states with the major concentrations in Oklahoma, Texas, Kansas, Illinois, Kentucky, West Virginia, Pennsylvania, and New York. These wells leak methane, contaminate groundwater and create community safety risk. These were only the wells that were documented, there are many thousands more that never were recorded.

Man's existence is in question, extinction of our way of life lurks, but if we are smart and do now what should be done, we may be able to extend our time frame. We have been spending earth's assets at an alarming rate over the last two hundred years. There is a limit; we have just so much clean air, clean water, heathy forest, vibrant oceans, and tillable nourishing soil. As they are diminished, so are we and our time frame is reduced.

Microsoft, The Web: As reported by Reuters: Coal-fired electricity in the United States is expected to be higher this year compared to 2020 due to soaring natural gas prices. The US Energy Information Administration said it expects 22% more coal-fired generation than in 2020.

AOL, The Web, Associated Press, 10/21/2021: Fossil fuel plans by many nations of the world would far overshoot desired climate goals. A new report by the UN Environment Program found that many governments are still planning to extract double the amount of fossil fuels in 2030 than what would be consistent to keep global temperatures' rise below 1.5 degrees Celsius. Climate experts say the world must stop adding to the total existing amount of greenhouse gas that only can be done now by drastically reducing the burning of fossil fuels. The report found that most oil and gas producers and even some coal producers are planning on increasing production until 2030 or even beyond. It also found that the group of 20 major industrialized and emerging economies have invested more into new fossil fuel projects than in clean energy since the start of 2020. The report of more than 40 researchers examined 15 major fossil fuel producing countries.

USA Today, The Web, 10/9/2021: Nearly 60 million Americans are living in drought-stricken areas in the Western US. Extreme drought, which last year covered 25% of the area leaped to almost 60% this year (2021). Agriculture uses over 90% of the water in western states. Yuma, Arizona grows 90 percent of all leafy greens during the winter months receiving almost all of its water from the Colorado River. Its average rainfall is about 2.5 inches annually.

Lake Mead's electric generating capacity has been reduced to 66% of its usual output due to low water levels, and Lake Powell could stop producing electricity entirely by January 2023 if the present dryness continues. Taylor Hawes a twenty-year water attorney and director for Colorado River programs for the Nature Conservancy said that this is likely not a drought, but the new normal. "Climate change is water change: too much, too little, the wrong time and the wrong location."

According to the 2020 census, three of the top 10 fastest growing states are Colorado, Utah, and Arizona. California added 2.4 million residents in the last decade. Where is the water to come from for these millions of people? As a country, we don't accept warnings from the experts, we seem to have to experience them for ourselves, but for climate change that is becoming very dangerous.

Microsoft, Citi 10/28/2021: Nearly 1800 companies have committed to the 2050 climate goals, but only 50% of those companies have set carbon reduction targets and only 10% of those companies have plans to deliver on their commitments. It is a big change for them to do this and the amount of necessary yearly investment will rise to $3.5 trillion dollars for the next decade. This will be almost impossible due shareholders and political objections.

Gizmodo, The Web, 10/8/2021: How can countries permit fossil fuel production to continue and increase while proclaiming that you intend to reach net-zero as some of the largest energy supply countries are doing? The United Arab Emirates, a country that dominates the world in oil and gas production, the United States, Canada, Brazil all have made net-zero pledges by 2050 or beyond. Its double talk and posturing knowing its thirty years away and who will remember or follow their progress by making sure they are fulfilling their pledge, and just as important who can and will enforce it? Until they start cutting fossil-fuel production on the supply side in the immediate future, it's nothing more than, "Blah, Blah, Blah," as the noted young lady Greta Thunberg, has so forcibly said.

The Web, 11/5/2021: Net-zero plans expect too much from nature. Net-zero pledges to protect the planet are increasing from companies, cities, and countries. But declaring a net-zero target doesn't mean they plan to stop their greenhouse gas emissions, far from it. Most of these pledges rely on planting trees or protecting forests or farmland to absorb some of their emissions. Question: can nature handle these expectations? Research says a big NO.

Extinction

Net-zero is the point at which all the carbon currently being emitted into the atmosphere is balanced by nature's ability to remove what is being emitted today. It has nothing to do with the existing CO2 already in the atmosphere or what is currently being added. According to the Intergovernmental Panel on Climate Change global carbon dioxide emissions need to reach net-zero by midcentury for the world to have even a small chance to limit warming to 1.5 degrees Celsius, to avoid the worst impacts of climate change. The amount of carbon to be removed will be just a limited amount by restoring and increasing nature's forest ecosystems and it cannot happen in time to help reduce the warming expected in the next two decades.

Research has reviewed Shell Oil's net-zero strategy and found that it includes offsetting 120 million tons of carbon dioxide per year, an amount they will still be emitting through carbon offsets by planting forest. It is estimated that to balance the 120 million tons, it will require the planting of around 29.5 million acres of trees. That's roughly 45,000 square miles. Is this possible or a sham? The review also included the net-zero pledges of three other oil and gas producers; British Petroleum, Total Energy, and ENI.

The report concluded that these three emitters' strategies for new forest would require an area of land twice the size of the United Kingdom. If the entire oil and gas industry adopted similar net-zero targets using forest, it could end up requiring enough land that is nearly half the size of the US, or one third of the world's farmland. Obviously net-zero offsets, like planting trees, to allow the continued emissions of fossil fuels is a huge sham, allowing offsets should be abandoned. These companies have no intention of meeting their pledges that they know are impossible, it's just a ruse permitting them to continue business as usual.

Research directs that net-zero approaches that rely on temporary removals of carbon to balance the permanent emissions will fail; trees die, are burned, and are harvested, releasing their stored carbon back into the atmosphere. The temporary storage of nature-based removals, limited land availability, and the time it takes for nature to begin the removals indicate that nature cannot compensate for continued fossil fuel emissions.

Microsoft, The Web, *Los Angeles Times*, 9/24 2021: "Renewable natural gas is the latest scam from the oil and gas industry." What is this renewable natural gas they are promoting? It's a methane gas that is not obtained by underground extraction. Rather, it's captured from ground-level methane-producing sources such as organic materials in landfills, wastewater, and manure from cattle. Equipment costing millions of dollars collects this methane and turns it into a form of natural gas that is used by consumers. It is an expensive process and it is not clean when it is burned. It is still methane, which has 80 times more warming capacity than CO_2 when released into the atmosphere.

Microsoft, The Web, 11/5/2021: Iraqis face an intensifying water crisis. Seven million people are at risk because of lack of water. The lands around al-Hama were once fields of orchards a few years ago have now become almost desert. Rising temperatures and low levels of rainfall have increased the severity of the drought. According to Human Rights Watch, more than 118,000 people were hospitalized in 2018 with symptoms related to water contamination. Farmers resorted to digging wells but found the groundwater was too salty. Diminishing water resources and water quality could lead to destabilization and conflicts between neighboring Turkey and Iran. According to the UN's migration agency more than 21,000 people were displaced in 2019 because of no access to clean water. Many villages were abandoned.

Microsoft, The Web 11/30/2021: Parts of the Artic could become dominated by rain rather than snow by 2060 or 2070 according to a report published in the journal *Nature*, an Artic Report Card; a study by the National Oceanic and Atmospheric Administration involving 133 scientists from 15 countries details how climate change has reshaped the Artic into a place that can have triple-digit temperatures, greater ice loss, and more melting of the permafrost, resulting in the increased release of warming gases.

USA Today, 12/7/2021: US sewer systems were not built for the effects of climate change. As more intense storms occur with increased rainfall, many communities with antiquated sewer systems that have a combined rainwater, snowmelt, and toilet waste piping system are having serious problems with sewage backup in their homes. The sewage and surface drainage systems were never designed to carry the discharge of the rainfall amounts that are now occurring. When the city's sewage system reaches its capacity, it overflows into the streets, flooding basements with raw sewage. Throughout the country there are 728 communities that have these combined systems. Most large cities have a dual system with separate drainage for surface water and sewage; they are not mixed.

Because these aging systems have not kept pace with new developments and population growth, the combined systems spilled 850 billion gallons of untreated raw sewage into open waters, rivers, and streams in 2004, the last time estimates were made. Rife with feces, pathogens, debris, and toxic pollutants, this is a series risk to human health and the environment. It will only get worse as climate change continues.

It has been determined that most of these combined systems exist in the same locations inundated with climate-driven rainfall extremes; the Midwest, Mid-Atlantic, and Northeast.

Their discharges contribute to pollution by contaminating drinking water and increasing algae blooms in rivers, lakes, and bays.

As an example, one week in early September 2018, a pair of severe storms swept across the Midwest and Northeast swamping many small communities that had the combined systems. Each city was overwhelmed, discharging a total of 330 million gallons of raw sewage-laden water into nearby rivers. Addressing climate change and its impacts on water infrastructure will be an expensive undertaking if we are to avoid continuing damage to the environment.

ARCTIC PERMAFROST AND METHANE GAS

Permafrost covers around nine million square miles in the Arctic. A team of scientists from Aberystwyth University warn that up to two-thirds of the Arctic's near surface permafrost could be lost by 2100 if the present warming rate is permitted to continue. Permafrost in the Arctic contains bacteria that—being frozen for a million years—has never been exposed to our current atmosphere nor to our antibiotics and we obviously have not been exposed to it.

The melting of the area's permafrost will influence every part of the planet as it releases large amounts of greenhouse gasses back into the atmosphere. As the Arctic thaws, it will release methane and nitrous oxide gas, a very powerful greenhouse gas. It is believed that there is a substantial source of nitrous oxide gas (N20) available along with the methane. There are estimates that over sixty billion tons of methane gas exist in the permafrost. If only a portion of this gas is released to the atmosphere, vast quantities of nitrous oxide, a greenhouse gas that is almost 300 times more powerful than $CO2$ for increased warming, will also be released.

Following a melt of the permafrost, these two gases could be emitted from a surface area covering almost one-fourth of the entire Arctic. A continual loop could occur as it is now with the Arctic ice sheet, where more thaws release more gas creating more thaws and releases. Because the nitrous gas has a greater potential for warming than $CO2$ over a period of a hundred years, it is considered a long-term greenhouse gas.

There is also nuclear waste frozen in the Arctic left over from 130 nuclear weapons tests by Russia from 1995–1996. When permafrost thaws, the land above sinks and changes shape. This can cause damage to infrastructure such as buildings, roads, airports, water, oil, and sewer pipe installations. In the shallow oceans, another massive source of methane occurs known as hydrates. These frozen crystals on the ocean floor collapse as the water warms, rise to the surface as bubbles, then release into the atmosphere.

10/12/2021, Russian Central Arctic, Reuters: The thaw of permafrost is crumbling buildings, threatening more than a fifth of Russian infrastructure and a critical part of its economy. Two thirds of the country sit on soil once thought to be permanently frozen, including most of its oil and gas infrastructure. In Yakutsk residences describe water pipes that regularly burst, holes occurring in buildings, and roads bucklering.

As Russia warms 2.8 times faster than the global average, the melting of Siberia's long frozen tundra is releasing greenhouse gases that scientists fear could frustrate global efforts to curb climate warming emissions. With permafrost covering 65% of Russia's landmass, the cost is already mounting; Russia could face $97 billion dollars in infrastructure damage by 2050. Across Russia more than 15 million people are living on permafrost foundations. In the near past everyone believed that melting permafrost would have an impact by the end of the century, but now we know that was wrong

Mines and commercial and industrial plants are experiencing increasing corrosive leaks and cracks. Pipeline support systems twist and bend when the supporting earth settles. The Russian government says that 40% of the buildings and infrastructure in permafrost-covered areas have already been damaged. "There isn't a single settlement in Russia's Arctic where you wouldn't find a destroyed or damaged building," said Alexey Maslakav, a scientist at the Moscow State University. Pipelines, storage facilities, electric power systems, and roads are increasingly in need of repair. As reported by the *Wall Street Journal* 10/5/2021.

10/7/21 Microsoft Start, Business Insider, the Web: Agriculture produces more methane gas than oil and gas emissions; about 30% of the increase in global warming since pre-industrial times can be attributed to methane. Its emissions are now growing faster than at any other time since record keeping started in the 1980s. Manure storage and livestock digestion are responsible for large quantities. According to the United Nations, methane gas has more than 80 times the warming power of carbon dioxide over a twenty-year period. It is also found in natural gas, decomposing vegetation, and exhaust from volcanoes. But the major sources are from the oil and gas industry, landfills, and most of all livestock. Fortunately, it takes only about a decade for methane to deteriorate in the atmosphere, that would be great if no more were added, but unfortunately much more is added annually than is lost due to its deterioration. Carbon dioxide on the other hand will stay in the atmosphere for hundreds of years.

In 2019, the combination of digestive activity from livestock and manure storage was the source of about 32% of human-caused methane gas in the United States. Human-caused methane could be reduced by as much as 45% in a decade. Will it be done and do we have ten years? But correcting human-caused methane release is only a small step. The big step is limiting or preventing nature's production and release of methane in the Arctic. If that is not controlled, forget about the cows; they won't matter.

Gizmodo, The Web, 10/26/2021. Permafrost could release long-buried pathogens: As permafrost thaws, it releases trapped greenhouse gases from the soil. Scientists warn that radioactive waste and dangerous bacteria and viruses also could be released potentially harming wildlife and humans. In a report just published by *Natural Climate Change*, they said, "It is important to understand the secondary impacts of these large-scale earth changes such as permafrost thaw," Kimberly Minor, a climate scientist at NASA's Jet Propulsion Laboratory. There is good reason to be wary of pathogens emitted from the ice. Over the summer, a team of scientists reported the discovery of 28 new novel viruses in a melting glacier in Tibet. Because of the length of time these viruses have been remote from humans our bodies may have no defenses. So far, 100 pathogens have been found in deep permafrost in Siberia. Ironically, new diseases may be the least of our worries if unchecked greenhouse gas emissions continue.

Heat Wave, 6/28/2021: A heat wave baking Siberia on June 20th saw ground temperatures reach 118 degrees; many Siberian temperature records were broken. This does not bode well for Russia's rapidly melting permafrost and greenhouse gas emissions.

In a recent scientific study, it was found that the permafrost melting is not fully accounted for in global warming projections, meaning those projections are likely too low making it harder for the world to curb global warming. People living in the Arctic today are suffering extreme disruption to their lives. They are seeing a humanitarian crisis; the ground is literally collapsing under their feet.

NOAA has reported that methane concentrations in today's atmosphere exceed 1,900 parts per billion, the highest amount ever recorded. The scientists say the seriousness of this finding cannot be overstated and are pointing to the perfect storm of a closed-loop effect where Artic heating due to climate change melts the permafrost releasing vast amounts of methane that in turn creates more heating.

Even if we reduce warming, the permafrost will continue to melt due to the present temperatures, and will continue to pump out carbon. To minimize permafrost carbon emissions, we must cut global emissions now. What countries are presently doing to fight global warming is not going to be enough to avert a world crisis.

The increasing frequent severity of Arctic wildfires emit large amounts of carbon not only from combustion but also by thawing permafrost. In 2020 these fires released 35% more CO_2 than in 2019. Those fires came amid a record-breaking heat wave in Siberia, where temperatures rose to 38C (104F), the highest ever recorded temperature in the Arctic Circle. "We don't have to wait 200 or 300 years for these large releases of permafrost carbon," said Katey Anthony at the University of Alaska. "Within my lifetime and my children's lifetime it will be seriously increasing."

National Geographic Magazine, 11/2021, The Thaw: In the small village of Nunalleg on the South West Coast of Alaska, archaeologists are in a hurry to discover the history of the Yupik people before it is lost to the sea. So far, they have recovered 100,000 carved wooden, bone and ivory artifacts that would have been lost forever due to the

Extinction

rising seas. Most all of these pieces were well preserved having been frozen in the permafrost since the 1600 hundreds. As the permafrost thaws, they are rapidly destroyed by moisture and exposure to the air.

Climate change is now harming the earth's polar regions and the melting results in the loss of artifacts from little-known cultures all along the Alaskan coasts and beyond in other parts of the Arctic. Rising seas and melting permafrost is causing the land to settle, threatening native villages and their heritage. When archaeologists began digging at the Nunalleg site in 2009, they hit the frozen soil 18 inches below the tundra. Today as they continue their work the ground is thawed three feet down. "One good winter storm and we could lose the whole site," said archaeologist Rick Knecht. All of this rich history would be gone forever.

THE OCEANS

Earth's oceans are home to most of earth's life and they also function like heaters and coolers; they are critical for our survival. More than 90% of the heat trapped by carbon emissions is absorbed by the oceans. The rate of heating of the oceans since 1986 was eight times higher than from 1960 to 1985. In 2020 the oceans reached their warmest temperatures ever recorded and five of the warmest years have all occurred since 2015. It is likely that the oceans now are at their hottest level in 1000 years and heating faster than at any time in the last 2000 years. Warmer seas provide additional energy to storms, making them more severe and frequent. There were a record 29 tropical storms in 2020.

Since the late 19th century sea levels have already risen by eight or nine inches. Much more sea level rise is imminent. In a report by the National Oceanic and Atmospheric Administration (NOAA), NASA the Department of Defense scientist project that in the next thirty years another 10" to 12" rise will occur along our coast. After that the waters will continue to rise by as much as a foot and a half or multiple feet this century. The ice sheets are just now getting warmed up and they will continue to warm and melt just like a large pile of snow slowly melts.

Today we have the advantage in measuring sea level rise by the use of satellites that beam radio waves to the ocean surface. This gives oceanographers a precise reading of sea level heights. Yearly sea level rise more then doubled from 1.4 millimeters over most of the 20th century to 3.6 millimeters by the early 21st century. From just the years 2013 to 2018, that number increased to 4.8 millimeters per year.

Two factors will cause sea levels to rise: Thermal expansion as the oceans absorb more heat. In 2021 the oceans were the hottest ever recorded by humans. In the past history thermal expansion has been responsible for one third of sea level rise. Melting ice sheets and glaciers: Nearly all mountain glaciers are melting along with the Greenland and Antarctic ice sheets. These ice sheets have lost large amounts if ice recently. Scientist again measure the loss by beaming lasers into the surface. The Greenland ice sheet, about three times the size of Texas, lost some 200 gigatons annually between 2003 and 2019 (a gigaton equals one billion metric tons). Antarctic lost some 118 gigatons each year. These two ice sheets accounted for two- thirds in sea level rise. In the future as they continue to warm, they will play a much larger role, there is a whole lot more ice to melt.

How fast and how much further melting will occur is really unknown. Humanity has never witnessed the Greenland and Antarctic ice sheet melting. During a warm period 125,000 years ago a massive amount of Antarctic ice melted rising sea levels by six the nine meters (18 to 27 feet). It may take several hundred years for this to happen but in geological time this is just a blink. Currently nothing can be projected that is going to stop or reverse the eventual rising sea.

In the Arctic due to the oceans' warming, the bright ice, that normally reflects heat back into the atmosphere, melts and is replaced by the darker ocean heat-absorbing water that heats rapidly, creating a constant loop of more heating than more ice melting. This feedback loop is just one of several reasons the Arctic is warming three time faster than the planet as a whole.

Microsoft, The Web, Amaza Labs, 10/18/2021. Because of the warmer seas, plankton are beginning to migrate and that could have catastrophic consequences. Plankton are the second most numerous species on the earth after bacteria. New evidence suggests that a movement towards the poles will occur if ocean temperatures reach 77 degrees Fahrenheit. Plankton are the major oxygen producers; they are an absolute necessity in the food chain. Without them most every single marine species would perish. The reduction or loss of krill, another one of the basic species of the oceans' food change, would affect all those who feed on krill and all those who feed on those that feed on krill, in effect everything.

The change in climate is reported to have killed 14% of all coral reefs in just ten years. Large scale coral bleaching events caused by elevated sea surface temperatures do the greatest damage to the reefs. Coral reefs require sunlight and are found in shallow water where the water can warm quickly and remain warm for extended periods. Coral is not a rock; it is a living organism.

Oct. 9, 2021, I.U.C.N. Report, The Web, "Our Suffocating Seas;" Ocean Deoxygenation:

Ocean deoxygenation is one of the less studied human-induced climate changes occurring but one of the most important. Its primary causes are the increased nutrient additions from rivers and land flows into the ocean, carrying sewage pollution along with nitrogen deposits from the burning of fossil fuels and agriculture fertilizers; this combines with the impacts of global ocean warming.

Oxygen loss in the oceans has alarming consequences for global ocean oxygen reserves, which have already been reduced by 2% over a period of just 50 years (1960–2010). Oxygen loss will impact marine ecosystems that humans depend upon. Even small reductions in ocean oxygen levels, when we are already near existing limits, can create complex biological changes. On a global scale, warming-induced oxygen loss is creating changes in nutrient cycling, species distribution and habitat availability. At the mouth of the Mississippi River, a large ocean dead zone, void of all life, exists where severe oxygen depletion has happened. There are also reports of oxygen depletion along the Pacific Coast of North America.

Yahoo News, The Web, 11/23/2021: The next great casualty of climate change could be global fishing stocks. "As scientists focus on climate, we believe that ocean oxygen levels are a pending casualty of global warming," according to a report in *Scientific America*. In the past, due to rising temperatures, portions of the ocean have lost 10 to 40 percent of their oxygen content and these percentages are forecast to continue to increase as more warming occurs. Rising ocean and fresh water temperatures have depleted oxygen levels; pollution and nutrient runoff have also been blamed for mass die-offs of fish this year in: Florida, California, Oregon., Montana, Louisiana, Virginia,

Pennsylvania, Missouri, Alaska, Washington, Idaho, Delaware, and Minnesota. As the amount of carbon dioxide increases, it warms the air and water. When a "heat dome" occurred this summer in the Pacific Northwest, raising temperatures that resulted in mass-die-offs of salmon and trout, it was estimated that millions of marine species along the West Coast of Canada were killed.

Water can absorb CO_2 and O_2 but only to a temperature-dependent limit; warm water holds less oxygen. This decreases the oxygen level and coupled with a large-scale die-off of oxygen—generating phytoplankton along with plastic pollution and industrial runoff—stresses ecosystems, asphyxiating marine life leading to the die-off.

Agoro, The Web, 11/18/2021. Ice sheet destabilized within a decade: Following the last ice age, there were periods when massive icebergs broke off from the Antarctic landmass. It took only a decade to initiate this tipping point in the climate system and then the ice loss continued for centuries. Studies of the sea floor sediments that were left by these large icebergs as they melted point to this rapid destabilization. Modeling studies of today's ice loss suggests that this loss also represents such a tipping point. The study leader, Michael Weber from the University of Bonn said, "Our findings are constant with a growing body of evidence that suggests the acceleration of the Antarctic ice mass loss in recent decades may mark the beginning of a self-sustaining and irreversible period of the ice sheet retreat and substantial global sea level rise." When will the destabilization of the ice sheet occur is unknown; it will depend on how much future climate change warming occurs?

New data from NASA's spacecraft reveal that sea ice surrounding the North Pole is thinner and disappearing more rapidly then previous realized. Using radar, the satellites can measure the ice thickness with a resolution of about a half -inch. What the new data shows is that the Arctic Ocean has lost about a third of its winter sea ice cover over the past 20 years. Scientist say that the ice that typically did not melt over the summer months has lost an average of about 1.5 feet in thickness just since the satellite began operating in 2019.

Microsoft, The Web, 12/15/2021: An Antarctic glacier the size of Florida is on the verge of collapse, scientists with the American Geophysical Union warned Monday. A nightmare scenario made worse by climate change that could eventually result in several feet of global sea level rise. The Thwaites glacier has been showing a proliferation of cracks across its surface. Fractures have developed that are allowing warming ocean waters to speed its destruction. It is estimated that the collapse could occur in the next three to five years.

There may be a considerable time lag; decades between the rise in global temperatures and the eventual maximum rise in sea levels before severe coastal flooding appears. The continual melting of the world's glaciers and polar ice caps will be slow but constant as they catch up with just the current rise of 1.2 degrees Celsius (2.2 F) but it will happen. The dye is cast; the inevitable has already started. The present amount of atmospheric CO_2 will be with us for hundreds of years and will obviously increase as the world struggles to reduce its carbon footprint.

A group of researchers from Climate Central have projected how extensively the waters will rise if the temperatures increase 3 degrees Celsius this century. The images of city streets turned to rivers and once-inhabited buildings sticking out of the water will be the realization of things to come. These buildings may be long gone if the world breaches 2 degrees Celsius. Long before an area is under water, it will face regular flooding from heavy rainfalls and storm surges that have already become more frequent and severe. These consequences will affect the developing world the most where large populations live in coastal cities. The study indicates that if greenhouse gasses continue at a high level, 50 major cities, mostly in Asia would need to defend against unprecedented amounts of flooding or face extinction.

Microsoft, The Web, 9/27/2021: The biggest abrupt rise in sea levels since the last ice age is occurring now. As the massive ice sheets of the last ice age began to retreat, having reached their maximum extent around 18,000 years ago, they added large quantities of fresh water to the oceans. This period of deglaciation saw an average rise in global sea levels of around 1cm per year. Around 14,600 years ago, this rate of rise increased dramatically. This event saw sea levels rise by about 20 meters (70 feet) in less than 500 years. Its probable cause was the partial collapse of the Antarctic and Greenland ice sheets.

Earth Week, I.R., 11/8/2021. Melt Floods: Increased runoff from the melting of Greenland's ice sheet is heightening the risk of global coastal flooding, according to new research. Scientist from Britain's University of Leeds say Greenland's runoff has risen by 21% over the past four decades, and has become 60% more erratic from one summer to the next.

They found that global heating has melted 3.5 trillion tons of ice during that period, which flowed into the ocean. Over the past decade alone, that melt has lifted sea levels by 0.4 inches. The study concludes the rising sea levels from that melt heighten the risk of flooding for coastal communities worldwide, and disrupt ecosystems of the Arctic Ocean.

National Geographic Magazine, 11/2021. Shrinking Ice: During the last 50 years, ice shelving along the Antarctic coast have calved into the sea, causing a loss of more than 11,000 square miles of ice. Warming seas accelerate the ice loss that seals and birds need for rearing their young. These are vital breeding grounds for penguins and two seal species that have long come to the Western Antarctic Peninsula to breed. Census of these nesting penguins record drastic losses, down 50% since 1970 that scientists link to global warming.

Krill anchors the food chain: The Western coast of Antarctic Peninsula is the hatchery for krill that sustain many species including migratory whales. But fishing vessels from Chile, China, South Korea, Norway, and the Ukraine now extract thousands of tons of krill each year to be used for products such as health supplements and fish food. The global demand for krill keeps growing; in 2020, 451 metric tons of krill were caught. How long can this last?

This icy world is imperiled: The Antarctic Peninsula is one of the fasted warming places on the planet. Air temperature during a heat wave in February 2020 reached a record 64 degrees Fahrenheit. Summer temperatures normally aren't more than a few degrees above freezing. In 2016 sea ice dwindled to its least amount since the 1970 when monitoring began. That's important because sea ice shelters the krill, the key to life in the Southern Oceans. Take away the krill and the entire ecosystem unravels.

These cities are sinking and could be gone by 2100: Miami, Florida; Venice, Italy; Jakarta, Indonesia; Mamba, India; and Bangkok, Thailand. Extreme sea levels will be more common around the world by the end of the century. Miami will be most vulnerable costal city in the world. Factors affecting these events include rising sea levels and, in the case of Miami, the porous limestone the city is built on will allow sea water to infiltrate drinking water supplies, increase high tidal flows, causing flooding and damage to infrastructure.

10/11/2021, Microsoft Start, *USA Today*, The Web: According to the National Oceanic and Atmospheric Administration, flooding is the most expensive natural disaster in the United States and has cost the nation one trillion dollars since 1980. One fourth of the US's "critical" infrastructure is at risk of flooding, the report warns. This includes utilities, airports, and emergency services such as police, fire, and hospitals. This is in addition to residential and commercial properties, state, and social infrastructure such as schools and government buildings. It includes all types of flooding, including rivers, coastal flooding, and storm surge from ocean storms. Our nation's infrastructure is not at present capable of resisting the level of flooding we face today let alone what we will face over the coming decades as the climate continues to change and storms and rainfall increase due to the change in climate.

A recent report in the journal *Nature Climate Change* describes how the Atlantic Meridional Overturning Circulation (AMOC) is at risk of slowing to dangerous levels or even stopping entirely as it has done before during extreme weather changes on the planet. The AMOC is a fancy name for the Gulf Stream that circulates around the Atlantic Ocean carrying warm water along the shores of Europe. Looking at a globe of Earth, you will notice that England is at the same latitude as Alaska. If it weren't for the warming effect of these currents, London would be an ice box and there could be drastic weather changes from northern Europe to central Africa causing severe cooling. The report points out how these currents have weakened over the last few decades. In 2021 it was found that the AMOC was weaker than at any time in the last 1000 years, causing alarm among scientists. The complex of warm and cold currents began to destabilize in the twentieth century and could cause severe weather chaos should it collapse.

If they should stop flowing, it will lead to an increase in storm activity, changing weather patterns, and food shortages in South America, India, and Western Africa. It could produce more rising sea levels along the North American eastern seaboard, forcing millions to flee their homes. Considering the AMOC is already starting to decline, it becomes a serious potential threat that could alter our planet in a matter of decades, the report said.

There is an interesting bit of history about these currents. Our country's first United States Postmaster, Ben Franklin, who traveled frequently across the Atlantic performing many valuable services for his new country, noticed that mail going from America to Europe always arrived two weeks earlier than the mail traveling back from Europe. On these voyages he performed many experiments and discovered and named the Gulf Stream current.

This was not the first report about the AMOC weakening. Another earlier report disclosed that these currents could weaken by 34% to 45% by the end of the century. One of the major causes of the weakening flows is the melting of the Greenland ice sheet and Arctic ice releasing vast quantities of cold fresh water. Cold fresh water being lighter does not sink, and that disrupts the balanced flow of the current causing a slowing or complete shutdown of the circulating system.

Because of current and future CO_2 emissions that are irreversible and are causing the continual rapid melting of the Greenland ice sheet, "this risk should be motivated to a high degree of caution," the report concluded.

Deadly microbial (algae) blooms have been repeated offenders of salt and freshwater extinctions during extreme warming events in the earth's past. The rise in microscopic algae inhabit the recovery of fresh water systems. The blooms deplete free oxygen and release toxins into the water and methane gas into the atmosphere. Similar events occur in salt water. This occurred during the Permian period of mass extinction that killed nine out of every ten species on the planet. According to this year's Intergovernmental Panel on Climate Change, the influence of humans is "unequivocal" creating conditions that favor the spread of these warm-water loving microbes. The effect of nutrients from water pollution, has led to a sharp increase in toxic blooms.

Earth experienced its worst mass extinction that was carried by a "toxic soup," a mix of accelerated greenhouse gas, high temperatures, and abundant nutrients and toxic algae. Tracy Frank, head of the department of geosciences at the University of Connecticut, said, "We're seeing more and more toxic algae blooms in lakes and in shallow marine environments that's related to an increase in water temperature and changes in plant communities, which are leading to increases in nutrient contributions."

USA Today, Excess Fertilizer Carried by Rains Poison Rivers and the Gulf, 12/9/2021: The production of corn and soybeans fuels one of the most insidious impacts of climate change fueled by the excessive runoff of fertilizer into the waterways of the country. Every year farmers apply tons of nitrogen fertilizer to vast areas of farmlands. As rain carries the unused fertilizer into adjoining streams, rivers, and lakes it increases toxic algae growth. The excess fertilizer eventually flows into larger rivers until it is deposited into the Gulf of Mexico creating a massive dead zone where life cannot survive. Increasing rainfall caused by climate change will only worsen the problem in the future.

Investigations have revealed that the extreme rainfall events of a warming climate caused three times as much fertilizer runoff as normal rain events. Among the most severe consequences of this runoff has been a lifeless dead zone that has been created in the Gulf of Mexico at the mouth of the Mississippi River, rendering 6330 square miles of ocean uninhabitable to life, according to recent measurements by the National Oceanic and Atmospheric Administration.

It is not just the Gulf of Mexico that is being affected. Fertilizer runoff also damages rivers and lakes. It contaminates drinking water, harms aquatic life, and sickens both people and pets. The algae bloom also emit methane gas that expands global warming. This emission creates another feedback loop where algae blooms create more climate change, that creates more rainfall, that then creates more runoff and then more blooms. Much of the problem is excessive application of the nitrogen. One county in Iowa had an average of 31 million more pounds of nitrogen applied to its corn crop than needed every year during the decade ending in 2019, according to data compiled by Iowa State researchers.

A study by the Monterey Bay Aquarium recounted in the journal of PLOS Climate reporting 150 years of ocean history found that the rising ocean temperatures including extreme ocean heat waves moved past the point of being irrecoverable in 2014. It points out how increasing heat is destroying ocean ecosystems. A hundred years ago extreme ocean heat wave events happened just 2% of the time but now they have increased to more then 50% of the time since 2014. That's what is happening today. What will be the effects in the future a hundred or two hundred years from now? We must learn to act and think on long term possibilities. Climate change is real. These occurrences will not disappear, they will be with us for all of our lives, the lives of our children and their children as we continue to warm the planet. It is insane for the world to persist down this path.

University of British Columbia-Science Section, The Web 10/19/2021: World heat waves could decrease the role of the oceans as a carbon sink. Researchers have found that the two-year ocean heat wave known as the "Blob" may have temporarily dampened the Pacific's "biological pump," that shuttles carbon from the surface ocean to the deep sea where it is stored for millennia. Canadian and European researchers, in collaboration with the United States Department of Energy Joint Genome Institute conducted large scale studies of the impacts of the heat wave on the Pacific Ocean microorganisms. Their observations suggest that it's not just larger marine life that is affected by abrupt changes in sea temperatures. "Heat waves may decrease the ocean's biological role as a carbon sink for fixed atmospheric carbon," said Dr. Seven Hallam, a microbiologist at the University of British Columbia.

The ocean is a huge global reservoir for atmospheric carbon dioxide. If marine heat waves reduce CO_2 absorption into the ocean, it will remain in the atmosphere as a greenhouse gas. Ocean microbes form the base of the marine food chain; they perform a very critical function. Very little is known about how they are affected by marine heat waves; but understanding their response can provide a vital sigh for the rest of the marine food web. "Marine heat waves are one of the big challenges of climate change," said Dr. Sachin, traveling lead author on the study at the University of Southern Denmark. "Knowing how they affect microbes—some of the smallest organisms on earth—will help us understand how heat waves will impact life in our future oceans.

Oceans have become so warm that temperatures are now too high near the equator for some marine species to live. An analysis of nearly 50,000 marine species between 1955 and 2015 found that many were moving away from the equator on a global scale, seeking cooler water that contains more oxygen.

Microsoft, The Web, Yahoo 10/31/ 2021: Sea level is already guaranteed to rise by at least 5 feet. Benjamin Stauss, a climate scientist, says based on the amount of CO_2 already in the atmosphere a 5-foot rise in sea levels will occur in the coming decades. We have already warmed the planet by around 2 degrees Fahrenheit, he said, "Think of it this way: If I dumped a truckload of ice in the middle of Phoenix, we all know it's going to melt. But it takes time to melt and the same thing is happening for Greenland's ice sheet and glaciers in Antarctica and those around the world." We have turned up the thermostat, but the melting has only begun and that's why we are already locked inn to extreme future sea levels. It's hard to imagine the long-term future of South Florida and other low-lying lands with the sea level rise that's already in the pipeline. Any additional warming will only add to more rapid rise.

ABC News, The Web, 10/31/2021: Hawaii's beaches are disappearing due to climate change. Rising sea levels and recent storm surges have been causing faster than usual erosion on Hawaii's beaches and shoreline. The costal issues that are related to climate changes are the "canary in the coal mine," a costal hazards specialist told ABC News. According to a recent report, three of Hawaii's major islands have lost roughly one-quarter of their beaches. Sea levels are also rising about one inch every four years, threatening 70% of the coast line. It was stated that in Maui alone, 85% of shorelines are eroding and beaches are narrowing as a result.

In the United Nations recent report "Code Red for Humanity" the islands could face a possible 3-billion-dollar loss in assets over the next few years, according to Maui Mayor Mike Victorino. Hawaii became the first state to declare a climate emergency. Victorino has accused fossil fuel companies of playing a major role in the climate change effects Maui has been experiencing. According to the Hawaii State Energy Office, the state is expecting to pay at least $19 billion dollars in losses from sea-level rise affecting condos, homes, hotels, and highways.

Yahoo News, The Web, 11/9/2021: Researchers studying the ocean at depths up to 6 km (3.6 miles) have found that climate change has a "worrying" effect on its ability to continue to lock away carbon. It has been revealed that if global temperatures increase to levels already predicted, the ocean will not be able to provide what is currently the earth's largest long-term carbon storage. One third of CO_2 in our atmosphere dissolves in the ocean. Billions of tons of carbon are buried in the deep oceans' muddy floor. This latest research shows that this cycle is disrupted by rising ocean temperatures. It also reveals that more of this buried carbon could be released into the atmosphere producing more heating. "The ecosystems are turning the carbon over faster when they are running at a higher temperature and they are going to deliver more carbon in the future."

A June 2021 report by Resilient Analytics and the Center for Climate Integrity concluded that Florida will likely face $76 billion in climate change costs by 2040, the *Tampa Bay Times* reported.

Extinction

"With sea levels rising at over a foot per decade, it's over," Harold Wanless, professor of geological sciences at the University of Mami said, pertaining to the eventual flooding of vast low-lying areas of costal Florida.

Associated Press; Portland, Maine, The Web. 11/2//2021: The warming planet is taking its deadly toll on seabirds that are suffering population declines due to starvation, heat waves, inability to reproduce, and extreme weather. Climate losses have hit albatrosses off Hawaii, Northern Gannets near the British Isles, and Puffins off of the Maine coast. Some birds are unable to find fish to eat as the ocean heats up, researchers have found. Common Murres and Cassin's Auklets that live off the West Coast of the US have died in large numbers from conditions scientists directly attribute to global warming.

One of the most serious threats to seabirds is a reduction of plankton and small fish in cold northern waters. Forage fish and plankton loss has led to mass die-offs of birds that have washed up by the tens of thousands on the Pacific Coast in recent years. "Seabirds are one of the most visible indicators of the health of our oceans," said Shaye Wolf climate science director of the Center for Biological Diversity. "These escalations of seabird die-offs are a big red flag that rising temperatures of the ocean is wreaking havoc."

"We cannot command nature except by obeying her."
– Francis Bacon

POLITICS AND REALITY

"There are two ways to be fooled. One is to believe what isn't true, the other is to refuse to believe what is true."

"Politics is the art of decision-making or lack thereof, mostly the latter."

"The pandemic certainly has revealed just how necessary immediate decisions can be politicalized. Now we are politicizing the very future of the planet."

"The Earth is the only world known so far to harbor life. There is nowhere else, at least in the near future to which our species could migrate. Like it or not, the earth is where we make our stand."
– Carl Sagan

The scientists can advise, warn, and plead as they have been doing for a long time and in many cases, they have been ignored, maligned, and accused of being extremists and fearmongers. They have had very little acknowledgments for their efforts and have been met with blank stares and complete denial of the emergency or of their concerns and supporting truths. In many cases, there has been a refusal that the problem even exists, claims that climate change is a hoax. It should be understood that climate change isn't something that is happening, it's something that's being done, and we are doing it. There are powerful people even now, who are deniers and are working hard to ensure that the world keeps burning fossil fuels.

To face off against the powerful political and financial interest, the only avenue scientists have is the road of public opinion and even that, until very recently, has many times been a dead end.

They don't have the power of the purse, lobbyist, nor political leverage to overcome the directed special interest and millions of dollars influencing decision makers who in the most part, are ignorant of what is occurring or are only interested in obtaining and holding on to power regardless of what is becoming more apparent as the world is burning up.

An international coalition of more than 1,400 scientists recently signed an initiative declaring that world leaders are consistently failing to cope with the main causes of climate change and the deepening climate emergency. Writing in the *Journal of Bio Science*, the group calls for the elimination of fossil fuel use, the slashing of pollutants, and the restoration of ecosystems.

Microsoft Start, The Web. 10/3/2021: The American oil and gas industries are fighting tooth and nail to kill or severely scale back the climate provisions of the president's Build Back Better Plan. "We're leaving everything on the field here in terms of our opposition to the anti-energy provisions," said Mike Summers, present and CEO of the powerful American Petroleum Institute (API) told CNN. Since August API has spent at least $423,000 on Facebook ads. Sommers said the API is working hard to get the clean electricity program taken out of the legislation. (And they succeeded!!)

Microsoft Start, The Web, 10/2/2021: Apple, Amazon, Microsoft, and Disney are among major companies backing corporate lobby groups that are battling a US climate bill. The US Chamber of Commerce, The Business Roundtable, and the Rate Coalition are three lobbyist groups opposed to the Democratic bill in Congress that includes significant moneys and measures to fight the climate crisis.

It will be the politicians and the moneyed interest that will determine the fate of the world and millions of its people. That's a very scary statement and let's hope it's not true, but as of today it's as close to reality as you can get. What we are considering is the slow destruction of life as we know it. Our habit of living beyond the laws of nature is no longer sustainable. Mother Nature delivers the rules and she is having her way. Extinction; Not tomorrow or next week nor next year or the next fifty or hundreds or thousands of years. She is not in a hurry. There are so many things to go wrong that it takes time. Extinction is a gradual, slow, painful process involving many different destructive outcomes over sometimes very long time periods, but once that process is accelerated through natural or human-caused events such as climate change and is set in motion, the clock starts ticking.

BBC News 9/28/2021, The Web: Doug Par, chief scientist with Greenpeace UK said "World leaders have done a terrible job of listening to the warning about climate change." He continued, "This year that has to change. We don't need more pledges, commitments, and targets. We need real action right here and now."

There are plans to tap a new oil field at Shetland, England. The government has said more oil wells can be drilled in the North Sea and there are plans for a new coal mine in Cumbria. If these projects are approved by the Oil and Gas Authority, drilling could start as early as 2022. The field is projected to produce oil and gas for twenty-five years. How can these and other similar projects be justified in light of the warming we are already experiencing?

Another example, BBC News, The Web, 9/28/2021: India lambasted the richer world countries' carbon-culling plans and long-term net-zero targets as "pie in the sky." Their energy minister Mr. Raj Kumar said "poor nations want to continue using fossil fuels and rich countries can't stop it." He pointed out that it was the rich countries that burned most of the fossil fuels that have caused the problems. They now want poor countries to stop, he said that is unfair. "The developed countries have created 80% of the carbon releases and there are even now 800 million people who don't have access to electricity. You can't go and tell them they have to go to net-zero, they have a right to develop, they want to build homes and have a higher standard of living. You have countries whose per-capita emissions are four or five or even twelve time the world's average. The question is when are they going to reduce their emissions?" That's what the world wants to know.

Microsoft, The Web, 11/5/2021: Indonesia appeared to back away from its pledges it made at the Glasgow conference. Its environment minister criticized the global plan to end deforestation by 2030 and to cut carbon emissions as "unfair and at odds with the country's development plans." Indonesia accounts for one third of the worlds rain forest. An activist with a local environmental group WALHI told Reuters news that Jakarta was "playing lip service" to tackle climate change while raising its production of coal. The country is the eighth biggest emitter of greenhouse gases in the world. It said it plans to phase out coal for electricity by 2056 and to reach net-zero carbon emissions by 2060.

Associated Press, The Web, 11/10/2021: China is offering no significant new goals for reducing climate-changing emissions ahead of the climate summit. China, one of the world's top emitters of carbon dioxide and other greenhouse gases said it aims to reach peak emissions of carbon, which they produce mainly through the burning of coal, before 2030. How much more CO_2 will be emitted to the atmosphere during those time periods? The country is aiming for "carbon neutrality, no net emissions" before 2060. Experts are concerned that pledges or emission targets and also financial support to help reduce emissions are coming in far too late and far too small and have questionable sincerity.

China's Minister Zhang Jianhua during a virtual event said that his country wanted "increased mutual understanding and mutual trust to work as one on the issue of climate change." Big words, little action. However, that desire to work together as one didn't stretch as far as the United Kingdom, with China declining an invitation to take part in a key climate development meeting for vulnerable countries.

Seven House Democrats from Texas, a fossil producing state, have raised alarms over their party's plan to combat climate change, saying it could cost thousands of jobs in the energy industry and increase energy costs for Americans. Were they really concerned for the country or their political future?

The Supreme Court just considered the Environmental Protection Agency's authority to curb greenhouse emissions from the nations power plants, a case that could defeat the Bidden Administration's plan to combat climate change. The justices will consider whether to limit the EPA's power to regulate carbon dioxide emissions from electric utilities the same day a United Nations science report pointed out a dire picture of global climate change. They are considering an appeal from 19 mostly Republican -led states and coal companies that contend that the EPA has only limited authority to regulate carbon output. Stay tuned for a decision.

These examples point out the difficulty of getting a consensus among the countries and people of the world to achieve meaningful changes in attitude and actions. Can it be done? There is the world's future and mankind at stake.

The United States just went through four years of inept leadership when nearly zero efforts were made to even acknowledge that climate change existed. From the very highest levels of government, it was called a phony hoax. Is it any wonder that people today are confused, that they ignore sound advice and form their opinions from lies and misinformation? We do not have any more excess years. If many of the American people respond to this more serious reality of an increasing warmer and changing world the same way they have responded to date (10/4/2021), to the current virus, by bickering, name calling, and in many cases, a reluctance to take even the simplest steps to save their own lives, how can we cope with something much more serious? There have been recorded cases of people as they struggled with their last breath, denying that they had the virous or that it even existed. That's the tragic reality of brainwashing and personal extinction.

Denali National Park, Alaska: Alaska is ranked as the fastest warming area on the planet and gets roughly one fourth of its spending from oil and gas reserves. Alaska's congressional delegation have strongly resisted efforts to block oil development in the Artic National Wildlife Refuge and they have supported expanding drilling in the National Petroleum Reserve. One of the state's senators, who is pushing for continual development said, "Climate change is real and it's human caused," as she pushes for new extraction projects. The senator crowed about her work to secure funding of federal money to fix a landslide and less than a week later scheduled a political fundraiser at the Anchorage home of the top Alaska executive of the oil company Conoco Phillips, the state's top crude producer. Even the Alaskan Governor has questioned the scientific consensus that human-caused emissions are driving global warming. As continued warming destabilizes other areas of Alaska's economy and threatens its infrastructure, the state elected leaders continue to promote oil development that is helping to fuel the problem. The single word that accurately describes these actions is "hypocrisy."

The only road into Alaska's Denali National Park, a major tourist attraction, was closed this August for a period of at least two years due to rock glacier failure, ice mixed with large amounts of rocky debris that is melting and has slid down more than a foot a day and taken out 300 feet of road bed. This has caused major disruption in the park's tourism industry that contributes $600 million a year to the state's economy. The park's managers have identified 140 more unstable slopes on the road, some of which are likely to also be affected by the continued melting of the permafrost. "It's highly likely that we will see mass movement events affecting the road in the coming decades" said Louise Farguharson, an artic geologist and research professor at the University of Alaska, Fairbanks. "This is not a one and done event," he said.

It is estimated that global warming could cost the state more than $500 million dollars a year over the next few decades. Some other events that are happening now:

1. The trans Alaskan pipeline that carries nearly 5% of the nation's daily oil production has been affected by thawing permafrost and flooding.
2. In the Bering Sea, federal scientists are reporting large declines in crab stocks.
3. In September Alaska's Native groups asked that a fisheries disaster be declared because of the collapse of the Yukon Rivers salmon population.
4. In response to permafrost thawing, one of Alaska's largest mines recently spent $19 million dollars on upgrading its wastewater system.

It is quite possible that the country will be further torn apart, continuing to be split along increasing ideological non-reconcilable interest that will make it almost impossible to reach a firm consensus as to what is necessary to be done about the increasing warming and the current destructive events that are occurring around the country and the world. Let's trust that we can come to our senses.

Yahoo, The Web, 9/21/2021: Climate change is causing high psychological distress among teenagers and young adults because of government inaction in the growing crisis. A recent international study found 45% of the young people surveyed said the issue is affecting their daily lives. The survey included 10,000 young adults and teenagers of ages 16–25 in ten different countries including the United States, Australia, India, Nigeria, and the Philippines.

It will be the young people of today and future generations who will carry the burden and shed the tears of this changing world in which they will have to live. It will be they who look back at us and scream: WHY? Fortunately, there is an awakening voice and it's reaching the world; their voices are being heard; they know it's their future, but they are like the scientists with no political power except what they can generate by their own hard work and personal sacrifices to arouse the public, no lobbyist, and no billions of dollars from special interest.

Unfortunately, today's children during their lifetimes will have to endure three times the disasters experienced by their grandparents. That's a hell of a burden we seniors have given to the children of the world because of our excesses. We can say we didn't know what was happening, and we didn't, but still it's hard to swallow knowing that some of their suffering could have been prevented.

Microsoft Start, The Web,10/16/2021, Examiner: According to a recent international study, 56% of teenagers and young adults believe humanity is doomed. The survey was conducted across 10 developed and developing countries including the United States. The findings point out the concern young people feel about a warming planet, they sense they have been betrayed by their elders: 83% said we have failed to care for the planet; 64% said their government is lying about the real impact of climate policies and nearly 40% said they are hesitant to have children due to the changing climate.

In an article in my local paper dated 9/30/2021 there was a perfect example as how far extremist politics has affected society and turned Americans against each other. When a doctor asked a COVID-19 patient if he would like to have a vaccination the patient loudly responded: "F _ _ _ NO!" and then proclaimed that he "would like to strangle the president for his effort to save lives by declaring a virus mandate!" How sick can we get? Most all health workers, nurses, doctors, and support staff once were saluted and praised as they should be for their unending dedication. Now, in parts of the country, they get threats. Sometimes even to their lives and those individuals making these loud threats become heroes in the eyes of their comrades. A nurse in Idaho was even afraid to go shopping unless she removed and wore something other than her hospital scrubs.

> "One of the saddest lessons in human history is this: If we have been bamboozled (lied too) enough, we tend to reject any evidence of the bamboozle. We are no longer interested in finding out the truth. The bamboozle has captured us. It is simply too painful to acknowledge, even to ourselves, that we have been taken. Once you give power to a charlatan over you, you almost never get it back."
>
> – Carl Sagan

Mass mind shaping propaganda is affecting this country today, attacking the very roots of our Constitutional Democracy. How long can our country maintain a reasonable degree of stability without a breakdown of society and the destruction of those foundations that have anchored us for over three hundred years? We are being separated as a people with ideologies foreign to us in the past. Obvious open lying is being accepted and practiced even at the highest levels of government and society. Known evident lies and more lies are being told and accepted as the truth even from our elected representatives. They are used as a means of impressing a segment of their unknowledgeable constancies regardless on the consequences that has on the country.

When society breaks down and a lie becomes the truth, and the truth a lie and is accepted by many people as the holy grail, watch out America, we are on a slippery slope towards a national tragedy. Hitler taught us that and lied his country, Germany, into a world war that killed millions of people.

> "The great mass of people more easily falls victims to a big lie then a small one."
> –Adolph Hitler

Have we learned nothing about the consequences of the Big Lie? Hitler told us the truth about the Big Lie. Did we listen? Are we listening now as we hear them over and over every day? Be careful America, your brains are being scrubbed. The young people of today did not experience this history; it would do well for them to be aware of the possible consequences of the actions of the Big Liars of today.

Can we maintain control of our economy? Our infrastructure is so fragile that our major industries can be held for ransom payments by foreign interests by someone merely typing keys on a computer. It happens, it's still happening, and will continue unless we resolve to take action to see it end. We have a health care system today that is stretched to its limits; major large cities are becoming unable to provide basic services such as trash removal, fresh water, health care, and police protection; murders and crime are rampant in many areas and mass shootings are almost a daily occurrence even in our schools. Some major cities' basic infrastructure, water, and sewer systems are over a hundred years old and need replacing. Roads and bridges are falling into decay.

What happened to the grand countries, empires, and the cities of yesteryear: Rome, Athens, Carthage, Babylon? Or the Moors, Visigoths, Iberians, the Phoenicians, and Greeks, Romans, the Egyptians, Persians, the Mongols, and the Sung Dynasty? In their times, they were the most powerful societies that ever existed, occupying vast areas of the known world. Many lasted for hundreds of years, some for a thousand years or more, but then they slowly disappeared. Why? They were all transitory things as we are. Few were overrun by wars and conquest. The majority died a slow death of their own making. Internal strife, bickering, crime, lust for power, a breakdown of society, moral decay, and fractions of dividing selfish interests were all the causes of the extinction of these great lands. What is happening in our country today? It takes a long time to rise to great glory and then to descend into the dust of history, never to recover.

> "It is historically true that no order of society ever perished save by its own hands."
> –John Maynard Keynes

During the glory years of Rome, its proud citizens marched throughout the known world. They fought and conquered, establishing an empire from England to Alexandra, Egypt. Their engineers built new wonders for the world: paved roads, water works, bridges, magnificent temples, colosseums, and public buildings, all surpassing anything the world had ever seen. Its people were industrious and proud, its early leaders for the most part were good for the country and its people. But then, ever so slowly in the later years, things began to change. They hired mercenaries to fight their wars and man the outposts of the vast empire. Internal strife split the nation into conflicts and rebellion. Games and pleasure became their desired way of life, they became fat and lazy and their resolve and respect for their country diminished. Where are we in this progression down through the ages? Do not be deceived, we are not forever.

Each generation has a group that wishes to impose a static pattern on events. A static pattern that would hold society forever immobile in a pattern favorable to the group in question. We must resist this at all cost for once the decay starts, it becomes embedded in a society and is almost impossible to reverse; history tells us this. To preserve and extend our very existence as a nation and a free society, there must be fresh air entering the halls of ignorance and intolerance. There can no longer be order and progress without personal and national discipline. Dogma can no longer be tolerated if we are to continue into the future; we must set aside our pettiness.

> "The dummying down of America is most evident in the slow decay of substantive content in the enormously influential media, the 30 second sound bite (now down to 10 seconds or less) and the lowest common denominator programing. Credulous presentation on pseudoscience and superstition by, especially, a kind of celebration of ignorance."
>
> – Carl Sagan

The leader of the United Nations Development Program, Achim Steiner said that we are in an "historical moment in time" with all the means to tackle climate change, but we are not making the decisions necessary to make it happen. Steiner said he is very worried; "The tragedy of this will be that my children, the next generation, they will no longer have the option because we will have moved beyond the point of no return. Because once we exceed 1.5 degrees Calais and continue to warm, it will take thousands of years to be able to reverse that, if it is even possible."

And that, in essence is the historical moment in time in which we find ourselves when essentially having the means to tackle climate change, but not finding it within ourselves to make it happen. It's very possible that our control of additional warming, because of the possibility of feedback loops; Greenland's ice sheet and the melting of the Arctic permafrost, are approaching a point where there is no possibly of changing their contributions to atmosphere warming.

The law of entropy holds that any system has within it, natural tendencies towards its own disintegration, randomness, and atrophy that will ultimately destroy the system unless counteracted by reinforcement of its rules holding the system together or new energy in support of the system is added. America's survival as a continuing political system is subject to this law and is in grave danger, not from forces beyond its borders but from the decay within itself that is now occurring.

Today some of our basic public institutions are under attack and public servants are becoming fearful in performing their tasks. Recently a school board meeting in New Hampshire was loudly harassed by repeated interference from a neo-Nazi group of extreme right-wing supporters called the Proud Boys, wearing swastika symbols. They were protesting COVID-19 mandates. These occurrences have become much more frequent throughout the country. There are many other instances where even doctors and nurses, school boards and election officials have been threatened. These are planned and organized attacks on our basic institutions seeking to disrupt society.

Microsoft, 10/18/2021: *Newsweek*. Senator Joe Manchin, who holds the key vote for passing climate change legislation said he will not support a provision in the bill for clean power putting at risk a central element of the legislation designed to fight climate change. Sen Manchin is from West Virginia, a leading producer of coal in the United States. The senator who has continually supported the coal industry just reported in his required financial disclosure statement that in 2020 he made $492,000 from shares he holds in a coal company. This amount represents more than twice his senator's salary. So, money talks and the world can go to hell.

The legislation that proposed to rapidly replace American coal and gas-fired power sources may now have to be scaled back because of his opposition. The Grant Town Power Plant releases more sulfur dioxide and nitrous oxide per unit of energy than any other of the state's coal plants. It is the dirtiest plant operating in West Virginia. He has made 5.2 million dollars from the company since being elected in 2010.

Yahoo News, The Web, 11/1/2021: It is highly possible that just one man, Sen. Joe Manchin, could be responsible for the watering down or the collapse of the Scotland Climate Change Conference. To appease the senator, the White House removed the Clean Electricity Performance Program (CEPP) from the bill that is before Congress that was to help fund climate controls. "Joe Manchin just launched a hand grenade at the Glasgow Conference," said Michell Mann, director of the Earth Systems Center at Pennsylvania State University, "Without a clean energy provision in the bill, the administration cannot meet its pledge of a 50% reduction in US carbon emissions by 2030. And as a result, the international climate negotiations could begin to collapse."

Yahoo News, The Web, 12/8/2021: A Yahoo News poll in October found that 67% of Republicans believe that climate change "is not an emergency." By contrast 78% of Democrats and 45% of Independents said it was.

Since we can't meet our reduction target how can we insist that other high emission countries, such as China and India, increase their contribution in limiting emissions. And without such agreements the world will remain on its current trajectory to blow past the 2 degrees Celsius into oblivion. We emit more greenhouse gasses than any other country in the world, we have to set a high standard and lead, but politics raises its ugly head and the earth and its people suffer.

Lompoc Record, The Web, 11/5/2021: It will take rapid action to slow the effects of climate change. Despite overwhelming scientific consensus, 18% of Americans still believe that climate change is not caused by human activities. Is this attitude any surprise when you consider that in our current US Congress, 30 US Senators and 111 members of the House (all from the same political party) have come out as climate deniers. (Can it be possible that the $62 million dollars they got from the oil companies might have anything to do with that?) With these people steering climate policies how is the country and the world going to make needed changes to reduce additional warming? This is not about politics as usual; it is a factual national threat to our security and worldwide human welfare. This issue should never be a matter of a political agenda.

Brussels, Reuters, The Web, 10/21/2021: Poland on Monday called for the European Union to cancel or delay parts of its plan to tackle climate change, warning that if "excessive burden" is put on consumers, they may reject the EU climate aims.

Los Angeles Times, The Web, 10/18/2021: NASA turns technology back towards the earth to focus on climate change. Its technology efforts are changing to study the effects of drought, fires, and the warming climate. NASA Administrator Bill Nelson told a group of scientists from NASA and JPL, "I don't want to be overly dramatic, but in truth this discussion is about saving our planet." (Authors comment: That statement is a real breath of fresh air; it's encouraging to know that someone of his standing is acknowledging that there is a serious problem.) There will be extensive studies with new radar and laser technologies to follow Earth's rapidly changing systems. It will provide a more precise look into everything that is happening. (Author: Please excuse me for being a little skeptical; we know what is happening and how to slow it down. We can study the problem and I welcome any efforts to provide clarity and practicality from NASA, which has the political clout, strong technologies, and public awareness. I would hope Mr. Nelson will continue to make that same statement in the public arena, and forcefully project the seriousness of the situation to all Americans; it's time for the truth and not politics.)

World leaders have been meeting for 29 years to curb global warming and in that time the earth has become a much hotter and deadlier place. Since 1992, 36 trillion tons of ice have melted. The worlds average sea level has risen about 3.7 inches since 1992. That may not seem like much, but it is enough water to cover the entire US to a depth of 11 feet (3.5 meters), University of Colorado sea water researcher Steve Nerem calculated. Wildfires have more than doubled. From 1983 to 1992 wildfires consumed an average of 2.7 million acres a year. From 2011 to 2020 the average was up to 7.5 million acres.

The Seattle Times, The Web, 10/29/2021: What will come out of the world climate summit in Glasgow, Scotland? This is the largest meeting and the twenty-sixth since the first one was held in 1992, seeking to stabilize greenhouse emissions and their danger to the climate. Have we learned or accomplished anything during those 29 years? Did anything change? Emissions continued to grow and the world continued to get warmer? Will this meeting be any different, will we be able to control the dangerous warming before reaching 1.5 degrees Celsius that most climate scientists say is a critical turning point?

Extinction

Tipping Points: As the world heats up there is a risk that the planet will reach "tipping points" where the earth's systems cross a threshold triggering irreversible warming impacts. When these points might be reached is uncertain. Droughts, reduced or excessive rainfall and continued destruction of forest through deforestation could see rain forest collapse, releasing more CO_2 into the atmosphere than their ability to store it. Or warming Arctic permafrost (already happening) could cause long frozen biomass to decompose, releasing vast amounts of carbon emissions; or excessive ocean heating could cause the destruction of that ecosystem. That's is why it is so important to control fossil fuels emissions now so we don't exceed one or more of these critical tipping points.

Warming to 2.7C would deliver unlivable heat for parts of the world across the tropics and sub-tropics. Biodiversity would be enormously depleted; food scarcity would increase and extreme weather would exceed most urban infrastructures capacity to cope. If we can keep warming below 3C we likely will remain within our adaptive capacity as humans in some parts of the world, but at 2.7C the world would experience great hardships. Remember, this could all happen within just a hundred years.

From a new report by the Quincy Institute for Responsible Statecraft, warns: "This is a risk that no longer can be ignored, that climate change will escape from human control altogether. Because of a set of positive feedback loops—Greenland's ice cover and the Arctic's permafrost. In this scenario 3 degrees Celsius of warming would spin out of control to 4 or 5 degrees. By such point the earth would have returned to its state 55 million years ago when the entire planet had a tropical climate and the sea levels were more than 120 meters (over 360 feet) higher than at present," says the report.

Microsoft, Citi, The Web, 10/28/2021: Nearly 180 countries have committed to the 2050 climate goals, but only 50% of those companies have set carbon reduction targets and only 10% have plans to deliver on their commitments. It is a giant step for them to do this and the amount of necessary yearly investment will rise to $3.5 trillion dollars annually for the next decade. This will be almost impossible to do under the pressure of shareholders' objections and political demands.

Reuters Foundation, The Web, 11/9/2021: Do carbon cutting promises actually add up to reducing emissions? Many countries and companies are pledging to cut their carbon pollution to net-zero. But those pledges do not mean the world is on its way on actually cutting emissions. Many such pledges do not depend on actually reducing emissions but rather on paying others to try and suck them up like planting trees. This is true of fossil fuel company's, oil- and gas- producing nations and other large emitters such as meat and dairy farmers. These carbon offsets, as they are known, are just another gimmick along with net-zero that allows these entities to continue business as usual.

Reuters, 10/29/21: As the climate conference in Scotland works to banish the use of coal, Asia is building hundreds of power plants to burn it. These new plants will emit 28 billion tons of carbon into the atmosphere. That's not far off of the 32 billion tons of worldwide CO_2 emissions from all sources in 2020. Why is controlling the burning of coal so important? There are several types of coal and their carbon content varies from 60% to over 90 %. As they are burned, that carbon goes directly into the atmosphere and remains there for hundreds of warming years.

New York Times, The Web, 11/1/2021: On Sunday leaders from the G20 conference who represent the world's biggest coal producers agreed to the first steps to weaken the use of coal in the future, but they fell far short to sufficiently address climate change. In a statement they said they would end financing of coal power plants to overseas countries, but the statement made no mention or commitments on the curbing of their use of coal domestically.

Moving the world's biggest economies away from burning coal is vital to hold within the 1.5C temperature target. Unfortunately, there are powerful countries that rely on coal. The time for setting "long-term goals is over" and pledges don't mean anything without action. More important than any promises countries make about 2050 is what they do between now and 2030. During the next eight years the world's biggest problem of all—coal burning—has to be seriously addressed. The single greatest cause of climate change is the burning of coal. More than any other pollutant, with the possible exception of the Arctic permafrost release of methane gas, coal has the power to defeat us in the battle to control temperatures from rising to catastrophic Earth-destroying levels.

Gizmodo, The Web, 11/1/2021, The scientists are terrified: A new Nature Survey shows leading climate scientists expect catastrophic impacts in their lifetime driven by rising greenhouse gas emissions. The survey from *Nature* involved querying the researchers who put out the major climate report, "International Panel on Climate Change." That report indicated that this is the most important decade in human history, one that will play a major role in how severe the warming will be for generations to come. Six in ten of the respondents to the survey expect the planet to warm to at least 5.4 degrees Fahrenheit (3 degrees Celsius) by the end of the century, which would be disastrous.

Udangudi, India: The giant Udangudi power plant is one of the nearly 200 coal-fired power plants under construction in Asia; including 95 in China, 28 in India with another 20 in the pre-construction stage, and 23 in Indonesia, according to data from US non-profit Global Energy Monitor (GEM). These plants will burn millions of tons coal for at least 30 years. They will produce planet-warming emissions for decades in the face of many countries reducing the amount of their coal-burning capacity.

More than 90% of coal plants being built around the world are in Asia. In China, 1000 coal plants are in operation and almost 240 more are planned or under construction. Together, coal plants in the world's second largest economy will emit 170 billion tons of carbon in their operating lifetime, more than all global CO_2 emissions between 2016 and 2020. Total global coal consumption is set to continue to increase where new projects are under construction. In South and Southeast Asia, coal-burning capacity will rise by 17% and 26% respectfully. Australia, where coal is a vital source of revenue—18 billion dollars per year—Keith Pitt, resource minister said, "While the market exist, Australia will look to fill it."

The fate of the planet will be negotiated in Glasgow, Scotland: In 2015 at the Paris climate talks almost every country in the world signed an agreement to limit global warming. What came out of those agreements signed six years ago? In the years since heat trapping emissions continued to rise at a rapid pace, the CO2 emitted into the atmosphere measured this year has risen to a record high of 415 parts per million. The Paris agreements aimed to limit global warming this century to less than 2 degrees Celsius. Now after six years later at this conference, countries and companies are pledging the same thing, contain global warming to 2C. This will require massive shifts away from the use of fossil fuels.

In the Paris conference these countries did agree that they would set more ambitious targets in the future to limit their emissions. Whether they will actually do so will be tested at the Glasgow Conference; it may well be their last opportunity.

If the US elections in 2022 shift power again to the "do-nothings" in Congress all bets are off the table for the near future to obtain progress in addressing climate change. It could be years before a breath of common sense is available. What happens now, first in Congress and then in Glasgow will shape the countries around the world commitments and actions. It's not a stretch to say that the future of our planet as we know it is at stake.

11/2/2021: French President Emmanuel Macron noted that the world's biggest polluters do not have policies in place to keep global warming within the 1.5 C target. A flurry of commitments has come from countries since the talks started, ranging from combatting methane leaks from oil and gas infrastructure to stopping deforestation. But one key thing is missing; an explicit and credible plan to end fossil fuel extraction and use. Without that, the world continues to play with fire. There is simply no way for the world to meet the 1.5-degree Celsius goal without winding down the fossil fuel industry as rapidly as possible.

We are talking a 78% drop in coal use and production; a 37% drop in oil and a 25% drop in gas as primary forms of energy, all the while increasing nuclear capacity by 59% (almost impossible) and renewables by an astounding 430% in nine years. Again virtually impossible.

I.R. Climate Warnings, 11/1/2021: The world is now on track for 2.6 degrees Celsius warming by the end of the century based on current pledges by world leaders to cut emission levels, according to a report from the United Nations. This report is another thundering wake-up call. How many more do we need? "The emission gap is a result of a leadership gap," UN Secretary General Antonio Guterres said. "The era of half measures and hollow promises must end, leaders can still make this a turning point to a greener future instead of a tipping point to climate catastrophe."

Government leaders face two choices in the Glasgow meeting. They can sharply cut, not with windy pledges but with firm action, greenhouse gas emissions now and help their own communities and other countries survive what is becoming a hotter, harsher world or they can accept the fact that humanity faces a bleak future on this planet and stick their heads in the hot sand and do little. So many countries at the conference are hacking at the small branches; when are they going to dig up and attack the roots of the problem?

In an interview, Bill Gates said partisan politics hurts the climate change battle. He said, "Sadly, the US is one of the worst in the issue of being partisan in nature. In the US, fighting climate change is a political issue and it can't be. We can't have a climate strategy where you have some parties in power that do a lot, but when you have other parties in power everything stops. Climate change has to be attacked consistently, not depending on which political party holds the White House."

Pledges without a serious commitment to end fossil fuels are worthless. As examples, the United Arab Emirates has pledged it will get to net-zero by 2050 but still plans to increase production and pump out more oil. The US has said it will cut emissions by 50% over the next decade while letting new pipelines go into operation and asking for more oil production. The United Kingdom is getting ready to approve a major new oil development in the North Sea. Many of the largest producers of fossil fuels have expressed skepticism about the International Energy Agency reports. There can be no substitute for winding down fossil fuel use as fast as possible. So far, the world leaders have failed to make these pledges a reality or take any decisive action to wind down production and use of the most dangerous products on Earth: coal and oil.

We are now entering a "heat age" in which temperatures and sea levels will be slowly rising decade by decade until the world becomes unrecognizable. There could also be more surprises. Nature is unpredictable, never more so when undergoing extreme times of change. We have no choice; reduce the burning of fossil fuels or face even worse consequences. Humans must learn to live in partnership with the earth, otherwise it will move to a new state in which humans may no longer be welcome.

We cannot treat global heating and the destruction of nature as separate problems. All living organisms, including us, greatly influence the global environment. The composition of Earth's atmosphere and temperature of its surface is regulated by the biosphere, by life. The planet is self-regulated, like a living organism. Two genocidal acts, suffocation by greenhouse gases and the clearance and destruction of the rain forest have caused changes on a scale not seen in millions of years.

Microsoft, The Web, 11/18/2021: Deforestation in Brazil's Amazon rain forest soared 22% in one year undercutting President Jair Bolsonard's pledge that his country is curbing illegal logging. In arial surveys and satellite studies a record of 13,235 square kilometers (5,110 square miles) was cleared in just one year, (2020–2021) an area 17 times the size of New York City. What the evidence shows is that the government has allowed the acceleration of the Amazon destruction.

Microsoft, The Web, Reuters, 11/7/2021: What's the difference between 1.5 degrees Celsius and 2 degrees Celsius? Scientists have told us that crossing the 1.5C threshold risks unleashing far more severe climate change effects on people, wildlife, and ecosystems. Each of the last four decades has been hotter than any decade since 1850, when climate records were first recorded. There never has been such a rapid warming in only so few decades that is affecting every inhabited region across the globe.

For every small increase in global warming, extreme changes become larger. Heat waves will become more frequent and more severe. An extreme heat event that occurred once per decade without human influence, would happen 4.1 times a decade at 1.5C of warming, and 5.6 times at 2C, according to the UN Climate Scientist Panel. Let warming spiral to 4C and such events could occur 9.4 times a decade, or almost every year.

Ice, seas, and coral reefs: At 1.5 C there is a good chance the collapse of Greenland's and Antarctic ice sheets could be prevented from collapsing, holding sea level rise to a few feet. But blow past 2C, and the ice sheets could collapse with sea levels rising up to 10 meters (30 feet). It is uncertain how quickly that could happen. Warming to 1.5C would destroy 70% of coral reefs but at 2C, 99% would be lost, destroying fish habitats and all species that rely on reefs for food and livelihoods.

> James Lowell: 1819–1891, "Blessed are the horary hands of toil! Once to every man and nation comes the moment to decide—in the strife of truth with falsehood for the good or evil side."

> "What we need to do is develop a new relationship with the natural world and its animals. If we don't somehow get together and create a more sustainable greener economy and forget this nonsense that there can be unlimited economic development on a planet with finite resources and that the GOP isn't God's answer to the future, then it's going to be a very sad world that we leave to our children and grandchildren."
> – Jane Goodall, 87-year-old famed primatologist.

Abraham Lincoln: 1809–1865, "If destruction be our lot, we must ourselves be its author and finisher. As a nation of free men, we must live through all times or die by suicide. There is no grievance that is a fit object of redress by mob law."

CLIMATE SUMMIT MEETING

"It has sometimes been observed that what leaders do for their people today is government and politics. But what they do for the people tomorrow, that is statesmanship. I, for one, hope this conference will be one of those rare occasions where everyone will have the chance to rise above the politics of the moment and achieve statesmanship."
– Queen Elizabeth II

In November 2021 at Glasgow, Scotland the representatives of 200 countries of the world met for the twenty-sixth time to try to come to an agreement to limit future warming of the planet. Their goal was to establish emission reductions of carbon dioxide to maintain future global temperature increases to no more than 1.5 degrees Celsius. They were charged by humanity to act this time, after twenty-five previous tries; to arrive at firm binding commitments to limit the increasing threat to the world posed by the continued release of excessive greenhouse gas emissions into the atmosphere.

What did they achieve? Was there a real sense of urgency and understanding for the task they must perform to save the planets very life from collapse? Did they listen to the scientists this time, who for years have predicted the severe weather, flooding, destructive fires, heat waves, mega-droughts, rising oceans, and warming sea's the world is experiencing today?

Accomplishments of the Summit:

New rules were proposed to limit future emissions of methane gas from oil and gas drilling wells. The United States and more than 90 countries signed a pledge to reduce methane emissions by 30% below the 2020 level by 2030.

New rules were also proposed to work with farmers and ranchers to promote "clean- smart agriculture practices" to reduce methane on farms. The US also issued a plan to conserve forests. More than 100 world leaders at the summit have committed to reverse forest loss and land degradation by 2030. This was the summit's first major international agreement. The US and other United Nations members have committed to net-zero greenhouse emissions by 2050.

India pledged to cut its greenhouse gas emissions to net-zero by 2070. China has pledged to hit net-zero by 2060.

Leaders of the world's biggest economies agreed to stop funding coal-fired power plants in poor countries outside their own boarders. A new US and European Union trade agreement was announced that would crack down on "dirty steel," that sends carbon emissions into the atmosphere.

The United Arab Emirates, one of the world's largest oil producers and Saudi Arabia announced it intends to reach net-zero gas emissions by 2060. Saudi Arabia announced that it will plant 450 million trees (in the desert) and rehabilitate huge swaths of land by 2030. The agreement did state that big carbon polluting nations have to come back and submit stronger emission-cutting pledges by the end of 2022. The Bangladesh plan envisions boosting renewable energy, making agriculture more resistant to climate change, and finding solutions in nature such as restoring mangroves to protect its coast from cyclones and erosion.

China and the United States announced an agreement to work closely together to fight climate change.

"Men do not and cannot and hopefully will never think alike, hence each must yield a little in order to avoid conflict, to avoid bickering. Man and woman must meet together and adjust their differences, this is compromise. He who stands unyielding upon a principle that is wrong is often a fool and often bigoted and usually is left standing alone with his principles while other men adjust their differences and move on."
– Louis L Amour

Failures, Disappointments, and Excuses:

"Man can hardly recognize the devils of his own creation. He has lost the capacity to foresee and forestall, he will end up destroying the earth."
– Albert Schweizer

First, we must understand that the world is locked into today's climate conditions. There is no going back; we must learn to live with the warming circumstances the world has already created and adapted to what is being added every day as carbon emissions increase. The carbon that is in the atmosphere today and any additional amount that is added will be there for hundreds of years. Our only possibility is to try to maintain and control those increases today at a level that doesn't fry the world in the future.

And the future does not end at the end of this century that so much of today's climate planning is based on. The future is the life of the planet. How will today's decisions and actions affect the planet for the coming centuries and millenniums? Man's modern existence on this earth has only been for a blink in time, we are babies and if we want to continue to grow up, we had better start paying attention.

Ahead of the talks, the United Nations had set three criteria for success, and none of them were achieved. The UN criteria included pledges to cut carbon dioxide emissions in half by 2030; contributions of 100 billion dollars a year in financial aid from the richest nations to the poor nations; and ensuring that half of that money went to the developing world to help them adapt to the worst effects of climate change.

Wealthy nations blocked a proposal to set up a new fund to help poor countries adapt to climate change, instead agreeing only to initiate a "dialogue" on the issue in future talks.

"The needs of the world's vulnerable people have been sacrificed on the altar of the rich world's selfishness," said a representative from Africa.

Glasgow, Reuters Report: China and Saudi Arabia are among a group of countries seeking to prevent the UN climate deal from including language that opposes fossil fuel subsides. The US envoy, John Kerry told the summit that trying to curb global warming while governments spend hundreds of billions of dollars supporting the fuel that causes it was "a definition of insanity." Promises ring hollow when the fossil fuel industries still receive trillions of dollars in subsidies.

New York Times, The Web, 11/14/2021: Negotiators struck a climate deal, but the world remains far from limiting warming. The new deal will not, on its own, solve global warming. Its success or failure will hinge on whether world leaders follow through to cut greenhouse gas emissions. The talks underscored the complexity of trying to persuade scores of countries, each with its own economic interests and domestic policies, to act in unison for the common good. Herding cats would be easier.

The detailed plans that governments have made to curtail fossil fuel emissions and deforestations between now and 2030 will put the world on a pace to warm by roughly 2.4 degrees Celsius this century, a disaster in the making. It remains to be seen if countries will follow through; there are no sanctions or penalties if they fail to do so.

The final deal is "not in line with the urgency and scale required," the environmental minister of the Maldives, an archipelago of low-lying islands in the Indian ocean that could be flooded within three generations.

The former Irish President said, "the pact represents some progress but nowhere near enough to avoid climate disaster. People in the future will see this as a historically shameful dereliction of duty."

AOL News, The Web, 11/12 21: The UN Climate Conference has resulted in many new pledges to reduce greenhouse gas emissions, but they still fall far short of the goal to keep temperatures below 1.5 degrees Celsius. An independent scientific analysis studied all the nations' plans to reduce pollution and found that the world is still on course for between 1.7 C and 2.6C of warming. We must remember these are only pledges for the future, not firm actions necessary today. Talk is no longer cheap. Pledges are just words until put into action. How many of those delegates making these pledges today will be alive in ten, twenty, thirty, or forty years? Will those who follow honor them?

Report: UN Climate Pledges Not Enough: The United Nations climate summit has made some "serious toddler steps" toward cutting emissions but far from the giant leaps needed to limit global warming to internationally accepted goals, two new analyses and top officials said.

This month's summit has seen such limited progress that a United Nations Environment analysis of new pledges found they weren't enough to improve future warming scenarios. All they did was trim the "emission gap"—how much carbon pollution can be spewed without hitting dangerous warming levels according to the review.

The analysis found that by 2030, the world will be emitting 51.5 billion metric tons of carbon dioxide each year, 1.5 billion tons less than before the latest pledges. To achieve the limit first set in the Paris climate accord, the world can only emit 12.5 billion tons of greenhouse gases in 2030, just eight years away.

"It is clear there is a massive credibility gap that casts a long dark shadow of doubt over the national pledges," the report states. "This is a critical decade," Claire Fysono, head of the climate policy team at Climate Analytics, told Yahoo News. "If we don't cut emissions by 50% from now until 2030, we really start to put 1.5C out of reach. A

UN analysis estimated that emissions will rise by 16 % by 2030 while the IPCC finds they need to go down by 45% in that time frame.

Some other results: There was no firm restrictions on the production of coal, oil, and gas nor were there any controls established for their burning and continuing to add emissions to the overheated atmosphere. India insisted that the wording for the use of coal be changed from "phase out" to "phase down" for the single largest source of greenhouse emissions. India, has long been a blocker on climate change controls.

Nation after nation complained that the talks, and that's all they seem to be, did not go far enough or more importantly, fast enough to reduce and control emissions. The Swiss environmental minister said the change from "phase out" to "phase down" will make it harder to limit the warming to 1.5C (2.7F).

"Today, the climate is warming, the animals are disappearing, the rivers are dying, and our plants don't flower like they did before. The earth is speaking, we have no more time," Txai Surui, 24, an Indigenous climate activist from the Brazilian Amazon, told delegates.

Although there were some measures adopted to reduce and control methane emissions nothing was said about nature's release of the Arctic methane; its control and importance. Plugging holes in pipes and oil rigs leaking methane is certainly warranted, but it is a tiny insignificant amount compared to the vast amounts waiting to be released in the Arctic. Those releases have already started and they can only possibly be controlled by the immediate and substantial reduction in greenhouse emissions. We don't have enough duct tape to plug that area.

Government leaders at the summit face two choices, Patricia Espinosa head of the UN climate office said. "They can sharply cut greenhouse gas emissions and help countries survive what has become a hotter, harsher world, or we can accept that humanity faces a bleak future on this planet." At the Vatican, Pope Francis urged the crowd gathered in St. Peter's Square: "Let us pray so the cry of the earth and its people," are heard by the summit participants.

The Wall Street Journal: The summit at Glasgow underscores the disconnect between the rhetoric over climate and what the world's publics are willing to do about it. Climateers adopt the rhetoric of the Apocalypse even as they consume fossil fuels as before because they know modern society and development require it. The world's climateers could do everyone, including themselves, a favor if they stopped pretending that they can alter the climate and thought more about adaptation and energy innovations. Alas, it's easier to make false promises and demand income redistribution. There can be no climate alterations, we must live with what we now have.

The world's citizens have already seen and felt too much of climate change to tolerate further platitudes or empty promises. Glasgow, if nothing else must be a forum for the hard truth that the earth faces going forward and whether nations are truly equipped to do something about it.

Scientists have made the math very easy. According to Reuters analysis of the findings, the earth can absorb only an additional 500 billion tons of greenhouse gas emissions without warming beyond 1.5 Celsius. The nations of the world today, led by China and America emit 50 billion tons a year.

The Biden Administration is planning to sell oil and gas leases on huge tracks of public land in the US West, despite the Interior Department's conclusion that doing so could cost society billions of dollars in climate change impacts. About 20% of the US energy-related greenhouse gas emissions are extracted from government-owned lands. Wyoming has the most land up for new leasing at roughly 280 square miles. A federal judge has just ordered the Biden administration to offer a massive new oil and gas lease in the Gulf of Mexico. The lawsuit filed by Republicans, was responsible for the reversal of a policy by the current administration that canceled the drilling leases allowed by the previous administration. He had no choice.

Abu Dhabi, United Arab Emirates energy ministers and others from across the world met on Monday, after the conference, and stressed the need for continued investments in fossil fuels just days after these same nations joined about 200 countries in accepting a compromise deal aimed at limiting rising global temperatures and curbing greenhouse emissions. They argued that over 60 billion dollars annually will have to be invested in the oil and gas industry until 2030. The US administration, while rallying nations to shift away from burning fossil fuels, has simultaneously called on OPEC to increase production.

From the book *Silent Spring* by Rachel Carson

"We stand now where two roads diverge. But unlike the roads in Robert Frost's poem, they are not equally fair. The road that we have long been traveling is deceptively easy, a smooth superhighway on which we progress with great speed, but at its end lies disaster. The other fork in the road—the one 'less traveled by'—offers our last, our only chance to reach a destination that assures the preservation of the earth."

REFLECTIONS

Where do you go when there is no other place to go?
How do you eat when the land is dry?
What do you do when your children are starving?
What do you do when you can't breathe the air?
What do you do when there is no water to drink?
How do you sleep when the nights are too hot?
How can you hope that life will get better?
When will you laugh and smile again?

There are people in the world today that are living those questions.
What of the future for others?

A poem by: Warsan Shire
Later that night
I held an Atlas in my lap
Ran my hand across the whole world
And whispered softly, where does it hurt?
It answered: everywhere, everywhere, everywhere.

SOME OF THE HURTS

Loss of Arctic Sea ice; melting of Greenland's ice cap; flooding in Tuvalu's nine Pacific Islands; extreme city heat, heat islands on land – buildings and other man-made objects; oceans heat islands; 23 bird species gone extinct; forest fires, Western US, Mediterranean basin, Amazon, Siberia; salmon deaths – Bethel, Alaska due to high water temperatures; disappearance of salmon – Yukon River; Oregon declares disaster relief for salmon fishery; Canada, Frazer River, salmon population collapsing, British Columbia spending $600 million dollars for relief; Klamath River – warm water fish die-off; Audubon Society said that unless warming is controlled, 2/3 of the US bird population is in danger of going extinct; Hawaii, warm seas are causing the bleaching and death of coral; the death of more than a thousand manatees this year (2021) in Florida.

Average global temperatures for Sept. 2020, 60.75 degrees, hottest ever recorded; heat waves, nine out of ten highest since 2000; oceans oxygen loss; ocean seabirds die off – Tufted Puffins; oceans acidification; drought in Southwest US; Lake Mead and Lake Powell record low water levels at less than 30%.; Lake Meads electric generation capacity reduced to 66%; Lake Tahoe – low water no longer flows out of lake into the Truckee River; record warming of the Great Lakes; warming of 60 lakes in the Northern Hemisphere; disappearance of African glaciers; Peru's melting glaciers; South America Parana River lowest since 1941; melting of Pasterze glacier, Austria; fish and marine species contaminated with plastics effecting the oceans biodiversity; 134% increase in flood disasters; possible Gulf Stream circulation change; recent CO_2 measurements in the atmosphere, highest in 3 million years.

Displacement of hundreds of millions of people from Africa, Central Asia, South America, Eastern Europe, and the Pacific; desertification in Spain and the Gobi desert; drought, Chennai, India; dying trees in Lebanon; water shortage in Saria and Lebanon; decline of the Monarch butterflies; Turkey's Lake Tuz dries up, killing thousands of flamingoes; sharks and ocean rays – 71% decline; bird migration disruptions; possible migration of ocean plankton; climate-related health problems; permafrost melting; damage to Russian Serbia infrastructure; French beekeepers worst harvest ever; Iraqis face water crisis – seven million people; disappearance of Hawaii's beaches; Madagascar's famine; deadly algae bloom increasing due to warming water and sewage runoff.

And to top this off, in a recent poll only 50% of Americans view climate change as a threat.

Extinction – Webster's Dictionary:
1. The state of being extinguished.
2. The fact or state of being extinct: dying out as a race, species of animals.
3. Putting an end to: coming to an end, destruction, annihilation.
4. Extinct – being at an end, no longer in existence.